What People A
Don Gossett's Mini.

CW00497703

"Don Gossett is a mighty man of faith. We are to be power-houses for God, and Don Gossett teaches you how."

—Marilyn Hickey
Marilyn Hickey Ministries

"Whenever this man of God writes, I read. Don Gossett has an anointing to stir up and enlarge people's lives. My life is one testimony of his powerful and transforming ministry."

—Senior Pastor Dr. Roge Abergel
World Harvest Church
Van Nuys, California

"Don Gossett's teachings from the Word have truly revolutionized and shaped our lives and ministry. The victories and successes we have experienced are largely attributed to his impact on our lives. He is truly a spiritual father and a friend to us, and we are eternally grateful to him."

—Pastor Jim and Rosie Parker
Living Word Christian Center
Spokane, Washington

"Don Gossett's walk with God has been a remarkable journey that will inspire faith in all who hear him in person or read his anointed writings. He is gifted in his ability to communicate the benefits of confessing the Word of God."

—*Pastor Holmes Williams, D.D.*
The People's Cathedral
Barbados

"Don Gossett has blessed the Christian world for over fifty years with his dynamic, faith-filled message of Jesus Christ's complete salvation, deliverance, and healing. This book, like his previous writings, will ignite the spark of faith within us to trust Jesus for all of our needs."

—*Reverend Dr. Jerry Lynn*
Reach Out Fellowship
Albany, New York

"I was first introduced to the ministry of Don Gossett in 1976 while in Bible college. His book, *The Power of Your Words*, made such an impact on my life that I have ordered hundreds of them over the years to give away. Don is truly a modern-day hero of faith, and my church enthusiastically supports his world evangelism. Don's wisdom, experience, and revelation have been some of the greatest blessings in my life."

—*Pastor Glen Curry*
Pillars of Faith Christian Center
Industry, California

LIVING
WITHOUT
FEAR

DON GOSSETT

WHITAKER
HOUSE

Unless otherwise indicated, all Scripture quotations are from the King James Version of the Holy Bible.

Living without Fear

(previously published with the title: *How to Conquer Fear*)

Don Gossett
Bold Bible Missions
P.O. Box 2
Blaine, WA 98231
www.dongossett.com

ISBN: 978-1-64123-143-5
eBook ISBN: 978-1-62911-108-7
Printed in the United States of America
© 1981 by Don Gossett

Whitaker House
1030 Hunt Valley Circle
New Kensington, PA 15068
www.whitakerhouse.com

This book has been printed digitally and produced in a standard specification in order to ensure its continuing availability.

ACKNOWLEDGMENTS

In presenting this book, *How To Conquer Fear*, I wish to acknowledge David Wilkerson for permission to quote from his writings. Also appearing here are quotations from my books: *Fear Power, Fear Not, Cold Feet and a Yellow Streak*, and *How You Can Rise Above Fear and Live in Victory.*

For many reasons, I wish to convey my gratitude to T. L. and Daisy Osborn; the late Dr. E. W. Kenyon; Dr. Norman Vincent Peale; Bob Whitaker; Vicki Mlinar; my five children, Michael, Judy, Jeanne, Don and Marisa; and my wonderful staff.

My warmest thanks and devotion are given to Joyce, my loving wife. Together, we have lived many of the struggles and victories written in those, pages.

All praise and glory belong, to our heavenly Father, who has made me, "more than a conqueror through Christ who loves me."

—*Don Gossett*

CONTENTS

INTRODUCTION:
FEAR HAS NO PART IN MY HEART

Former president of the United States, Herbert Hoover, once said upon returning home from a world tour,

"The dominant emotion everywhere is fear. This applies to every part of human activity: finances, industry, farmers, workers, thinkers and government officials. This was a strong statement from such a highly esteemed man, and it is a fact that sadly still holds true today.

When I consider the amazing number of people in all walks of life who are obsessed by some inward fear, I feel the responsibility as a servant of God to declare that you can be free from fear!

Just what is fear? Fear has been defined as the expectation or apprehension of evil.

Now within limits, fear is a good thing. We cannot live either our natural or our spiritual lives without it. A child will burn himself unless he has a proper fear of fire. A pedestrian will be knocked down or killed unless he has a respectful fear of traffic. A man cannot a successful Christian unless he respectfully fears God, *"The fear of the LORD is the beginning of knowledge"* (Proverbs 1:7).

It is a healthy trait to fear both danger and sin.

But there's another kind of fear which is very unhealthy. This is the fear which brings torment. (See 1 John 4:18.) The fear that causes you to always expect the bad. This fear is an insidious monster that, if it takes its full course in your life, will produce misery, defeat, bondage and destruction.

Fear creates nervous breakdowns, sleeplessness, and oppression in your prayer life, bondage in witnessing. Fear can lead to an urge to commit suicide. It can be manifested in stinginess toward God in your giving. Fear can truly be defined as the expectation of bad.

Satan wants you to have this diabolical spirit of fear, which expects and magnifies evil, failure, sickness, danger and worry. I realize the tremendous significance of a statement made by Dr. Len Jones of Australia, "Fear is the devil's second name!"

Many people do not recognize fear when it poses as prudence, caution and discretion. But we must come to grips with this and realize that these are really fears disguised by the devil. Satan will use every subtle device he can find to hinder the good things of God. I believe that fear is the greatest spiritual hindrance to keep people from completely yielding themselves to God and enjoying a rich, abundant life in Jesus Christ.

I challenge you! Do not knuckle down to fear. Resist fear and you will overcome. *"Resist the devil and he will flee from you"* (James 4:7).

Affirm this power poem with me: Fear has no part in my heart! Now, let's learn how to *conquer fear!*

1

COLD FEET AND
A YELLOW STREAK

When I arrived in Saskatoon for our crusade, a tall police officer welcomed me to the city. Two nights later, this same man responded to my invitation to accept Christ. Since he bad told me he was a Christian, I was puzzled by his response in coming with those to receive Christ.

"What do you need?" I asked him.

"Brother Gossett, I heard you talking about cold feet and a yellow streak," he replied, "and that's my condition. In my Christian life and testimony, I plainly have cold feet and a yellow streak."

I gazed at this man towering several inches above me. I was forcibly impressed that physical stature has little to do with the spiritual condition of cold feet and a yellow I streak.

Multitudes of Christians have made a similar admission. But it's a real shame that any Christian should have cold feet and a yellow streak when God has made every provision for you to live free from this condition.

In my observation this is one of the greatest hindrances to being used of God.

WHAT IS COLD FEET AND A YELLOW STREAK?

It is the spirit of fear that comes not from God. (See 2 Timothy 1:7). It is *"the fear of man that bringeth a snare"* (Proverbs 29:25). And this *"fear hath torment"* (1 John 4:18).

It is a lack of confidence in Christ and the Bible that produces a spirit of timidity, reluctance and hesitation. And as long as one is oppressed in this manner, he will not be triumphantly proclaiming, *"I can do all things through Christ which strengtheneth me"* (Philippians 4:13). Nor will he shout, *"I am more than a conqueror through Christ who loves me"* (Romans 8:37).

It is a lack of courage that causes thousands to live weak, defeated, apologetic lives-far, far below their abundant privileges in Christ.

SOME WHO HAD
COLD FEET AND A YELLOW STREAK

The Bible is the divine record of great heroes of faith. But it also abounds with examples of those who displeased God and were useless to Him because of their cowardice and lack of courage.

In Numbers 13 and 14, God told Moses that the land of Canaan was theirs to possess. Moses sent twelve spies out to investigate the country. Twelve men walked together side by side, saw the same country, witnessed the same conditions. But ten of these men had cold feet and a yellow streak; two of them did not.

The ten spies, filled with fear and cowardice, brought about the downfall of the nation of Israel there. Disregarding the promise of God, they reasoned it was impossible for them to take the land. Two attitudes and words that characterize people who have cold feet and a yellow streak are "impossible" and "hopeless." But these are two words that must be eliminated from our vocabulary if we walk triumphantly by faith!

Only Joshua and Caleb were "bold as a lion" and urged the people to "fear not … the Lord is with us."

But ten of the men voted for defeat and failure; only two voted for victory and success.

The ratio is much the same today even among Christians… about ten out of every twelve believe in fear, failure, and lack and oppression, more than they believe in living free from fear and with the sure knowledge that "God is with us."

You can conquer when you go forth in the name of the Lord! But there must be an absence of cold feet and a yellow streak if you are to experience bold conquest.

God commands us to be *"in nothing terrified by your adversaries"* (Philippians 1:28).

This life of Victory through bold Bible living belongs to you. In the words of Ezra 10.4, I challenge you: *"Arise; for this matter belongeth unto thee: be of good courage, and do it!"*

Never again do you have to yield to fear and cowardice. Never again do you have to be reluctant in acting upon God's word.

⌐⌐

BREAK THE SILENCE

You have read this message silently up to this point. Now's the time to break the silence and begin to speak the following statements out loud.

"My God hath not given me the spirit of fear" (2 Timothy 1:7).

"The LORD is on my side; I will not fear: what man do unto me" (Psalm 118:6).

"I am more than a conqueror through Christ" (Romans 8:37).

"For he hath said, I will never leave thee, nor forsake thee. So that we may boldly say, The Lord is my helper, and I will not fear what man shall do unto me" (Hebrews 13:5-6).

"I have been made righteous in Christ. And the righteous are bold as a lion. I am bold in my faith, bold in my praises, bold in my prayer life, bold in my testimony for Christ. To be bold in the Lord means to possess real confidence, courage and the daring to do God's Word."

Now read these declarations again, slowly, forcibly, in faith, and add this one: "I am done with cold feet and a yellow streak. I can live free from fear every day. The Lord makes me strong and courageous. I am like David, fearless in the face of giants of oppression. Like Joshua, I daringly face my battles in the name of the Lord. And the more boldly I believe (act on the Word), the greater are my victories and success in the Lord!"

THE PRICE FOR COLD FEET AND A YELLOW STREAK

One of the shocking statements of the Bible concerning those who are doomed for eternity in the lake of fire includes the *"fearful"* (Revelation 21:8). This describes the moral cowards who are afraid to take their stand for Jesus.

This is a day for bold living. For men to arise and say, "As for me and my house, we will serve the Lord."

Most people who are filled with fear (cold feet and a yellow streak) are self-centered. They think of themselves, instead of Christ. Fear has torment, but perfect fear casteth out fear. (See 1 John 4:18.) When you are controlled by love, you will rout that cold feet and yellow streak because you are filled with concern for the needs of others.

I man who had a bad case of cold feet came to one of our services. I asked him to give a simple witness to his love for Christ and his faith in the Savior.

When the man arose to speak, it was nothing but a faltering series of apologies, with such declarations as, "I'm not much good at speaking in public," or "This is too hard for me, I just can't express myself before people." Finally, in exasperation the man sat down, succumbing again to defeat.

But this whole "testimony" was one of "I can't;" his attention was completely upon himself. "I, me, my and mine" are four key words that characterize those who have cold feet and a yellow streak.

But when love constrains us, fear is conquered. Why? Love focuses no attention upon self and the fear of what others think of you.

FEAR IS NOT OF GOD

Have you accepted Satan's foul gifts? Satan, not God, is the giver of fear. The Bible says, "*Every good gift and every perfect gift is from above, and cometh down from the Father of lights, with whom is no variableness, neither shadow of turning*" (James 1: 17).

God gives you good things, perfect gifts. And anyone who has been the possessor of fear knows so well that it is neither good nor perfect.

If you are fearful, you have accepted the gift of Satan. *"God hath not given us the spirit of fear; but of power, and of love, and of a sound mind"* (2 Timothy 1:7).

God gives you power, love and a sound mind.

Satan gives you fear, weakness, inability, resentment, a mind that is the cesspool of iniquitous, impure, defiling thoughts.

Refuse to have Satan's gifts. Tell the devil, "In the name of Jesus, Satan, I command you to take this old spirit of fear and depart from my life."

It is not the will of God for you to live a life of fear. James tells us to "resist the devil and he will flee from you."

The devil is the author of fear every time. Whenever you are fearful, you are giving place to the devil. The Bible commands, *"Neither give place to the devil"* (Ephesians 4:27).

The devil is a liar and a coward, so make your stand against him boldly, fearlessly, in the mighty name of Jesus.

~

THE SYMPTOMS OF COLD FEET AND A YELLOW STREAK

When you are ruled by fear and cowardice, you are governed by certain negative characteristics that are painful in their results for your life.

People who have cold feet and a yellow streak are *indecisive.* They can never make a clear-cut decision. They will try to spiritualize their indecision until all possibility of achievement is destroyed. Those who are indecisive permit others to do their thinking for them, to make their major decisions of life. They stay "on the fence," never being clear-cut about anything.

Bold decisions are a part of the Christian who lives as "more than a conqueror through Christ." Why? Because Jesus is made unto us wisdom from God. (See 1 Corinthians 1:30.)

Another negative trait of the person who has cold feet and a yellow streak *is over-caution*. This over-caution is a bad habit. Living boldly in the Lord is to acknowledge the Lord in all of your ways, to follow Jesus who is the light upon your pathway. But it is never to be surrounded by uncertainty, by worry, by doubt.

People like this are always looking for the possible failure in every undertaking. Their reason is their worst enemy because it is plagued by fear, and fear is of the devil...every time.

Remember your victories, and forget your failures. Focus your attention upon success in every situation. When you know you are right, go ahead!

Another negative factor in the life of one who has cold feet and a yellow streak *is procrastination*, putting things off until tomorrow next year, or some better time in the future.

Oh, how I've had to deal with those who are fearful, and those who postpone victorious and successful living to some future time. I've counseled with people who always feel that something will happen some time in the future that will miraculously prepare them for ministry, or for supernatural results.

These who are avoiding their God-given responsibilities are a sad lot. It is hard to sympathize with them. They compromise every time they have difficulties, instead of boldly fighting the good fight of faith.

Listen, difficulties come to all of us, but the victor learns to use them as a stepping-stone to advancement, to overcoming in Christ.

Procrastinators are always filled with alibis and excuses.

Learn to put up a stiff fight when pressures and problems would seek to overtake you.

HAVE A REBELLION

When we were preaching several years ago in French Canada in an open air crusade, the noise, distraction and interference of the first night service spelled certain defeat and disaster for our mission there. But God had equipped us for such combat the realm of the Spirit. We rebelled against Satan. We refused to accept defeat

Little passive, namby-pamby Christians would have Piously quoted Romans 8:28 and gone on, resigned to failure.

But not bold living Christians; that's what God wants us to be! We rebelled. We met God in hours of fervent prayer. We sent out requests for the prayer support of others.

Praise God, when we resumed that open-air campaign in downtown Montreal, all of the troublemakers and disturbers were gone. God had given us the victory!

In every situation where defeat seems to have the upper hand, that's the time to rebel against Satan who has come to destroy, to kill, to make of no effect.

SOME GOOD HONEST QUESTIONS

To overcome this spirit of cold feet and yellow streak, it is important to ask yourself some vital questions:

Do I associate with people who are fearful?

Are any of my so-called friends really my enemies, if they are fearful, negative, and faultfinding people?

If it is true that "birds of a feather flock together," is this why I am attracted to negative, fearful people?

Do I help people to overcome their worries by boldly giving them biblical answers, or do I permit others worries to bring me down?

Do I daily practice my rights as a Christian by living free from fear and doubt?

Do I seek to lift people to a higher plain of life, or do I permit them to lower my standard of living?

Am I known among my friends as a bold, triumphant Christian who takes my authority in Christ?

How do I react when I encounter some negative person who is filled with fault-finding, pessimism and doubt? Am I prepared for them?

Do I have definite purposes in life?

Am I an indecisive person?

Do I regard myself as a so-called *weak Christian?*

Am I often "in the clouds" of spiritual ecstasy and then often in depression?

What makes me grow most in the Lord and in the things of the Spirit?

Do I feel jealousy toward those who excel beyond me in life?

Am I one who seeks self-pity and sympathy?

Am I a person who finds fault with others?

Am I sarcastic in my relationships with others?

Even if you have answered yes to any of these questions, you can be set free from cold feet and a yellow streak-today!

2

THE FEAR OF MAN

The type of fear that vexes and captivates more Christian lives than perhaps any other fear is the subtle fear of man.

What a bondage this fear of man was to my young Christian life. I had been saved in a non-Christian family so sharing a Christian testimony in my home, to my school friends and on my job was a fearful experience.

The fear of standing up for Jesus was a real challenge for me. When I really said yes to Jesus, letting Him be Lord and Master of my life, the hardest battle I had was working on the job with a group of very ungodly, filthy-mouthed men who cursed repeatedly. In sincerity, I made a commitment, "Lord, "I'm not going to be ashamed of you or Your gospel." I memorized Romans 1:16, *"For I am not ashamed of the gospel of Christ: for it is the power of God unto salvation to every one that believeth."*

Then, I would go to work and lunchtime would come. I was determined to bow my head and thank God for the food I was about to eat, but it wasn't that easy. While the rest of the fellows would dive into their lunch boxes and start eating, I would just sit and look around to see if anybody was watching me. Sure enough, someone always seemed to be watching! For the first week it was really a struggle. I'd lift my hands to my eyes, covering most of my face, and bowing my head I'd whisper, "Thank you, Lord, for the food." The way I would rub my eyes they probably thought I had some kind of eye disease!

Well, praise God, I kept on reaffirming, "I am not ashamed, of the gospel of Christ,'" until, finally I got to the place where I could bow my head confidently and say, "Thank, you, Lord, for the food, in Jesus's name. Amen." Hallelujah! God really ministered courage to me.

The Lord doesn't receive glory in anybody being ashamed of Him or succumbing, to the fear of man. This life is so short. As the song says, "Only one life, it will soon be passed. Only what's done for Christ will last." It's a pity to live this life oppressed by the fear of man with all its consequences when God has made a way for us whereby we can be totally free from fear in, all areas of our life.

Being willing to be used of God in bold ministry for over 20 years has not been easy for me, but by the grace of God I have learned how to resist and overcome the fear of man.

"The fear of man bringeth a snare: but whoso putteth his trust in the LORD shall be safe" (Proverbs 29:25).

How often I experienced that soul-snaring fear of man! The word _snare_ implies a trap or an entanglement. The devil longs to keep us in his trap, entangled because of the fear of man.

Are you trapped and hindered in your Christian effectiveness because of tormenting fear?

Do you allow Satan to seal your lips when you would speak for Jesus, because of the fear of others?

Are you hesitant to be used of God in ministering healing to the sick, or casting out demons, because you are afraid of the opinions of people?

Do the blessed gifts of the Spirit lay dormant in your bosom because you are afraid to exercise these gifts, afraid of others' disapproval?

Are you hindered in your Christian ministry because you fear the opposition of your own family?

This fear of man is so prominent in its working against the Christian. It seals the lips, renders powerless anointed lives and keeps its victims tormented.

No more striking words are to be discovered in the Bible about the consequences of fearful living than these: *"Fear hath torment"* (1 John 4:18).

FEAR ENCOUNTER IN CHICAGO

I was ministering in the city of Chicago some years ago when I had one of the most dreadful fear experiences of my life. I was preaching each afternoon in the Coliseum on South Wabash in Chicago. Hundreds of souls were being saved in response to my salvation invitation given each day. These meetings continued for about ten weeks with glorious results.

One night after the service, I was at the back of the Coliseum near the bookstand. I saw a man there and felt in my heart a moving of compassion towards him. I walked up and extended my hand to him. The man rudely refused to shake hands with me and with a few unkind remarks left the Coliseum immediately. I was puzzled by his reaction but thought nothing more of it.

The next day, the same man returned to the Coliseum, and walked up to me. With a smile on his face, he apologized for his behavior of the previous night.

He explained, "I don't know what came over me, but for some reason I just wanted to kill you. "

I studied the man's eyes for a moment and then replied, "Well, I'm glad you've come back tonight where the Lord can help you with your problem."

A few days later, I met the man at a cafeteria, where I was having lunch. He was friendly, and I invited him to join me at my table. I talked with him, concerning how much the Lord loved him and wanted to bring deliverance to his life, and I urged him to receive Jesus Christ as his personal Savior. The man listened, but would not commit his life to Christ.

The next time I saw this man was on Roosevelt Road in Chicago. I was walking with my wife and two small children He rushed up behind me and began to swear at me vehemently. I was startled it his cursing and embarrassed that my wife and children were subjected to his language.

I stopped, turned to the man and ordered him to leave us alone. He shouted out a few more profanities and then went the other way.

A few days later, I was walking down Wabash Avenue enroute to my afternoon service. Just a short distance from the Coliseum, this same man was waiting for me between two buildings. Totally unaware of his presence, I suddenly was pounced upon and viciously assaulted by this man.

For a few moments I was so stunned by his blows to my face that I didn't realize what was happening.

The man was speaking even more viciously and violently than on our last encounter. As he moved toward me, threatening to cut my eyes out and kill me, I prepared to defend myself against his renewed assault.

As I listened to his flow of violent words, I became aware that he was speaking with a fluency that wasn't natural for him. In speaking to me before, he stammered and was hesitant. But now there was no impediment in his speech at all, just an unceasing flow of words.

The Holy Spirit revealed to me that this man was not speaking his natural words but was under the influence of a supernatural ability. Satan himself was controlling this man's words and actions.

Aware that this was not a matter of flesh and blood conflict but in the realm of spiritual darkness arrayed against me, I knew I must employ the Spirit's weapons instantly.

I spoke with authority, "In the name of Jesus Christ I rebuke you, Satan. I command your power in this man's life that is set upon my destruction to be broken right now. In the name of Jesus, you devils of hell, I curse you, and I command you to leave me alone."

Suddenly, as if some unseen force had grasped him, the man's arms fell to his sides and then, with a burst of speed, he began running down Wabash Avenue. As I saw him flee, he acted as if he were being chased by a dozen strong men!

I'm convinced that the power of the Lord was the unseen force causing this reaction and the triumphant results in that moment of near disaster.

TORMENTING FEAR

Even though there was subsequent victory in my experience in Chicago, for about the next ten weeks tormenting demons visited me regularly with their accusations and insinuations.

These demons of fear would speak to me, "Your God didn't protect you there in Chicago. He let you get viciously beat up. How do you know He won't let it happen again?"

I would resist these demons in Jesus's name and they would leave, only to return again at an unsuspecting moment.

The spirits of fear taunted me with these thoughts, "If God did permit me to get beaten physically in Chicago, and it could happen again."

So I would often brace myself for the attack of some unknown assailant. Walking down a busy street, I was suspicious of people who looked at me peculiarly, lest they would be Satan's instruments to attack me again. Even in our crusade services, I was on the lookout for satanically controlled individuals who might be instruments of destruction against me.

This harassment continued for about ten weeks, until finally, I came to grips with it boldly and defiantly.

I told the devil, "Satan, you are a liar. I know you are a thief, a destroyer, and you've come to kill. But I want you to know, devil, that greater is the One who indwells my life than all of your power that can be arrayed against me. In the name of Jesus, You tormenting demons, I dislodge you from my mind, and I command your power be broken once and for all. I bind you under the blood of Jesus Christ, for it is written, "In the name of Jesus shall ye cast out devils; nothing shall by any means hurt me; I overcome you demons by the blood of Jesus and the word of my testimony."

Praise the Lord, the Holy Spirit ministered a sweet and lasting victory. Never again was I to be tormented by this fear that beset me for those ten weeks. Years have passed and I still have this victory over the fear of destruction, the fear of calamity, the fear of physical harassment and the fear of man.

12 REASONS WHY YOU CAN BE FREE FROM THE FEAR OF MAN

Scores of times in the Word, God has appealed to His people in all ages to resist the fear of man. Carefully study the following references. These are the words of God spoken to His people. These words are for us today.

Get ready for a mighty release in your inner man as you meditate upon these truths. This is God speaking to us now.

As you read these commands, promises and holy challenges, get ready to shout your freedom! Prepare to arise in Jesus's name and be free from the fear of man.

1. *"Ye shall not be afraid, of the face of man"* (Deuteronomy 1: 17).
2. *"And the LORD said unto Joshua, Be not afraid because of them"* (Joshua 11:6). The same Lord who spoke to Joshua is speaking to you from the Old and New Testaments and by His Spirit today, "Be not afraid because of them."

3. *"And the angel of the LORD said unto Elijah, Go down with him: be not afraid of him"* (2 Kings 1:15). It is enlightening to discover how often the messages of the angels of heaven were exhortations to "fear not" and "be not afraid." If you meet an angel, likely he will urge you to fear not.

4. *"And I looked, and rose up, and said unto…the people, Be not ye afraid of them: remember the LORD"* (Nehemiah 4:14). What sound advice Nehemiah gave so long ago, and it is so good for today. Whatever or whomever you are facing, remember the Lord! Focus your attention on Jesus, remembering Him instead of the people you are fearing, their opinions or judgments. *"Looking unto Jesus, the author and finisher of our faith"* (Hebrews 12:2).

5. *"I will not be afraid of ten thousands of people, that have set themselves against me round about"* (Psalm 3:6). This was David's confidence expressed and often experienced in his life. If anyone could write with conviction on overcoming the fear of man, it was David! Knowing his experiences of being opposed by man with seemingly insurmountable odds, we can latch on to his words with great confidence.

6. *"In God have I put my trust: I will not be afraid what man can do unto me"* (Psalm 56:11).

7. *"Be not afraid of their faces: for I am with thee to deliver thee, saith the LORD"* (Jeremiah 1:8). How, prone we are to fear the countenance of man. What a battle I experienced in this area of fearing the faces, of people. My fearful efforts of public speaking were horrifying. Only

the Word of God set me free, when I could stand up without fear, speak to people and watch their faces without being struck down by soul snaring fears!"

8. *The LORD is on, my side; I will not fear: what can man do unto me?"* (Psalm 118:6).

9. *"Only rebel not ye against the LORD, neither fear ye the people of the land...the LORD is with us: fear them not"* (Numbers 14:9). Rebellion against the Lord is often a forerunner of fear. The Holy Spirit can be resisted, quenched and grieved, if we obey not the Lord, but rather give, place to the fear of man.

10. *"Fear ye not the reproach of men, neither be ye afraid of their revilings"* (Isaiah 51:7).

11. *"The LORD is my light and my salvation; whom shall I fear? The LORD is the strength, of my life; of whom shall I be afraid?"* (Psalm 27:1).

12. *"For he hath said, I will never leave thee, nor forsake thee. So that we may boldly say, The Lord is my helper, and I will not fear what man shall do unto me"* (Hebrews 13:5-6).

3

OTHER PHOBIAS

I have a friend, a psychiatrist from Washington, D.C., whom I met on the Island of Antigua in the West Indies. I spoke with this doctor about the fear of people

We discussed some of the results of the fear of man. He explained *androphobia* to me, the fear of man, as psychiatry defines it. He cited cases of *aphephobia* a manifestation of the fear of man. Aphephobia describes those who have "an aversion to being touched by men." He told me of patients of his who would not shake hands with other people because of this fear of man.

In our discussion at Antigua, this, doctor explained to me *gynephobia*, the fear some men have of women, also the fear some women have of men. The doctor was clear to define these phobias as the product of an outside force or spirit. Fear in any manifestation is not just a mental quirk. It's an actual spirit; yes, a spirit of the devil.

The doctor explained *gamophobia*, the fear of marriage. I remember ministering to a young man who told me he had been engaged to be married five times.

He said, "I want to get married. I know it is right. But when it comes right down to it, I am afraid of marriage!"

In the name of Jesus, I cast out this spirit of fear and soon the young man was happily married. His marriage has been a great success. But first he had to be delivered from gamophobia.

Satan has succeeded in inflicting these spirits of fear upon multitudes. The mental hospitals are filled with people who have given place to these foul phobias, until their lives were wrecked and ruined.

This fear of man is often seen in the fear called *misophobia*, a fear of dirt. The doctor from Washington, D.C., described case after case of those who have this phobia. He cited this example: a man who would not shake hands with anyone, lest dirt or diseases were passed on to him. He would hardly permit members of his family to touch him. He spent his time washing his hands; 50 to 100 times per day. Does that sound extreme? This is how captivating spirits of fear can be.

THE FEAR OF BEING POISONED

My wife and I know an outstanding couple in the Lord's work that are deluded by the devil by *toxicophobia*, a fear of being poisoned. It is clearly a spirit of the fear of man. At times they feel that God is revealing to them that the food set before them in a restaurant is poisoned, and they refuse to eat a bite of it.

These are people who know God but are snared by this fear of man and what man can do to them.

MY DELIVERANCE FROM LALIOPHOBIA

Earlier in this book, I made reference to the fear of man that beset me as a young man.

The doctor calls the fear of public speaking by this term: *laliophobia*. I had a bad case of it.

When the Lord Jesus laid His hand upon my life and called me into the ministry, I was assured by Him, but had toovercome some real fears.

After that unforgettable all-night visitation of God in my bedroom when I heard His voice and accepted His holy call, I shared the experience with my sister, Donnis, at about 1:30 in the morning. Donnis was the only member of my family who was saved at that time. We rejoiced and wept together.

Then I determined I would tell my dad when I heard him stirring in the kitchen the next morning.

About 6:30 I heard him downstairs so made my way down to tell him how the Lord had called me to preach the gospel, and that I had accepted His call.

Now, my dad had lived a rough life up to that time. The only thing I ever heard him say about the Lord was in curse language.

He was I man of the world, a thorough-going sinner who loved the bottle, gambling, infidelity and other vices.

When I told him what happened in the night, he walked over and looked me in the eye. Slowly he inhaled his cigarette smoke, and then blew it across the room, still not saying a word.

Turning to me, he said, "I don't see how you could ever be a preacher. You have always had trouble talking, even to one person. And to be a preacher, you have to do a lot of talking."

Certainly he sought to discourage me. He was dead set against the idea of my becoming a preacher.

There had hardly been a Gossett Christian, not to mention a preacher in this family!

But I knew the Lord had called me.

Faced with all of his opposition, I bolstered up courage to reply to him, "Dad, I know I can't talk well. But I do know the Lord has called me to preach, and, by His help, that's what I am going to do with my life...preach the gospel of Jesus Christ."

I had hoped my dad would understand. I wanted him to receive my announcement favorably.

Even though he didn't, I turned from the kitchen and went back up the stairs to my bedroom.

There alone I turned to God's Word, and my eyes fell on this Scripture, *"Fear thou not; for I am with thee: be not dismayed; for I am, thy God: I will strengthen thee; yea, I will help thee; yea, I will uphold thee, with the right hand of my righteousness"* (Isaiah 41:10).

How this passage nourished my heart! If God would be with me, I reasoned, I would have no need to fear. Hallelujah!

Within six months, my dad was saved by the grace of God and has never opposed my ministry since.

That morning on my knees, God delivered me from laliophobia, the fear of public speaking.

The fear of man has many phobias, such as *demophobia*, the fear of crowds of people (even in a church service!); or *claustrophobia*, the fear of being in close places.

Most decisive is this Scripture, Proverbs 29:25: *"The fear of man bringeth a snare: but whoso putteth his trust in the LORD shall be safe."* There is safety and deliverance in the Lord!

I invite you to examine this list of fears that you might be comforted with God's assurance that you can live free from fear, for fear shall have no part in your heart as a redeemed child of God.

Ailurophobia - fear of cats.

Algophobia - fear of pain.

Androphobia - fear of men.

Anemophobia - fear of winds.

Aphephobia - aversion to being touched by people.

Arachnephobia - fear of spiders.

Astrophobia - fear of thunder and lightning.

Autaphobia - fear of being alone.

Basiphobia - fear of walking.

Bathophobia - fear of falling from high places.

Batophobia - fear of high objects (towers, mountains).

Carophobia - fear of insects.

Claustrophobia - fear of enclosed places.

Coprophobia - repugnance to filth and dirt.

Cynophobia - fear of dogs, of getting rabies.

Demophobia - fear of crowds.

Doraphobia - fear of touching animal hair or fur.

Ergasiophobia – dislike of work, taking responsibilities.

Gamophobia - fear of marriage.

Gephrophobia - fear of crossing bridges over water.

Hemophobia - fear of blood.

Laliophobia - fear of public speaking.

Lyssophobia - fear of going insane.

Necrophobia - fear of death or dead bodies.

Nudophobia - fear of being seen unclothed.

Ophidiophobia - fear of harmless snakes.

Pantophobia - pure fear state.

Peccantiphobia - fear of committing social errors.

Pharmacophobla - fear of medicine.

Photophobia - fear of light.

Psychrophobia - fear of cold.

Pyrophobia - fear of fire.

Rhabdophobia -_fear of being beaten.

Scopophobia - fear of being observed.

Scotophobia - fear of darkness.

Sitophobia - fear of food.

Thalassaphobia - fear of sea voyage

Toxicophobia - fear of being poisoned.

Zoophobia - fear of animals.

"That he would grant unto us, that we being delivered out of the hand of our enemies might serve him without fear, in holiness and righteousness before him, all the days of our life" (Luke 1:74-75).

4

FEAR PRODUCES IN KIND

I was in Klamath Falls, Oregon, conducting a crusade at the First Assembly of God Church, where Silas Jones was pastor.

One day Pastor Jones and I were asked to make a house call, to pray for a blind man who told us this story:

"For many years of my life I had perfect sight. Yet even then, I had this fear within me that some day I would lose my sight. It haunted me often.

"Then came the time when my sight began to fade. My fears were enlarged. Doctors told me I would need glasses to aid my vision but nothing more serious. But this nagging, tormenting fear increased. I feared that I would not just stop at failing vision. I was grossly afraid I would completely lose my sight, that some day I would be in total darkness.

"And surely enough the day came when I completely lost my sight, and I have been blind here in my home for several years'" the man told us.

I was reminded of Job's experience, which contains an important warning for all of us. Job lost his health, his family, his possessions, his everything.

Job also, like the blind man in Oregon, was a victim of cruel fear. Listen to him explain his experience of great oppressions: *"For the thing I greatly feared is come upon me, and that which I was afraid of is come unto me"* (Job 3:25).

Why is fear so powerful? How can fear produce those things we do not desire?

We need to understand that fear is satanic. *"For God hath not given us the spirit of fear; but of power, and of love, and of a sound mind"* (2 Timothy 1:7).

When you, begin to fear, you are giving place to the devil. Satanic fear develops more fear. And the spirits of fear can literally torment, snare and captivate.

You must learn to deal with fear in its earliest stages, to resist it, cast it out; refuse to give place to it. This can be done through the name of Jesus, by the empowering of the Holy Spirit, upon the authority of God's Word.

Job testified that he greatly feared this thing. Small fears, if not checked, develop into great fears. The greater the fear, the more readily they develop.

The devil, who is a deceiver; works in subtle ways to brainwash people into accepting his evil works.

"LOVERS OF THEIR OURSELVES"

One of the signs of the last days is that *"men shall be lovers of their own selves"* (2 Timothy 3:2). This spirit is so prevalent today; surely we are living in the last times. And a manifestation of this spirit is the fear of ill-health, the fear of sickness. Most sick people are self-centered. That is why it is difficult to get people who are hypochondriacs healed, because they are self-centered. And selfishness is not the climate for victorious faith to be operative. *"Faith worketh by love"* (Galatians 5:6).

I constantly counsel with people who have a horrible fear of ill-health. They are always looking for symptoms of some kind of disease. They almost seem to enjoy imaginary illness, and they speak of it with relish.

These folks love to talk to you about their operations, their accidents, and their experiments with different diets, pills, fads, remedies, etc.

When you are filled with the fear of disease, you invariably concentrate upon disease, and that fear produces all kinds of sickness.

I read a statement by a prominent medical authority that most nervous breakdowns are caused by imaginary illness.

Get rid of that image of illness and begin to see yourself in the light of God's Word as a strong, healthy, vibrant person. Hold that image by confessing God's Word that declares, "By His stripes you are healed."

This fear produces self-coddling in your bid to get sympathy and pity. But hear me, sympathy and pity will never help you; it will never minister healing and health to you. It will only produce the very thing you fear.

～

NOT BOUND BY HEREDITARY LAWS

Very often I have counseled with people who became stricken with cancer, who have told me they feared cancer into being. The devil brainwashed them into believing that because other members of their family had cancer that they, too, would have it.

This same spirit of fear manifests itself in heart attack victims and other diseases.

While I acknowledge the power of the laws of heredity, I acknowledge a greater law, that is the law of life in Christ Jesus. New life in Jesus. Abundant life.

It is vitally important that we do not give place to fear. For the thing which we greatly fear can come upon us, and that which we are afraid of likely will come unto us.

Many people have a fear of flying. Yet statistics reveal how much safer per mile flying is than driving a car.

Fear makes its play in unsound thoughts, in the area of the mind. But God gives us a "sound mind" which learns to resist fear.

Fear a car wreck, and you could be opening the way for Satan to involve you in a car wreck.

Fear a cancer, and you could be paving the way to be afflicted with foul cancer.

Fear a heart attack, and satanic spirits can unquestionably produce a genuine heart attack.

The famous American physician, Dr. Alexis Carroll, states: "Fear is capable of starting a genuine disease. Many other medical authorities verify this fact. Job testified to it. The man in Oregon confirmed it.

This is why you must get rid of your fears, lest your fears destroy you.

Fear that your flight might result in your untimely death, and you could be giving Satan opportunity to do his worst destructive work.

Fear failure, and likely you will fail.

Fear the countenance of man, and you ensnare your soul.

Fear some sickness, and you increase the prospects of a deadly malady vexing your life.

Fear old age, and old age can be a terrible experience.

Fear, the loss of affection of your loved one, and you could be opening the way for opposing powers to assail.

Fear is no joke. It is a Bible fact. It is constantly verified by medical doctors and psychiatrists. Fear produces in kind.

There is power in fear. Power to torment. Power to snare your soul. Power to paralyze your potential, to render you ineffective, to handicap you in life. Power to produce in kind.

Remember that this fear is not a mental quirk, but an actual spirit that emanates, not from God, but from the adversary.

"For ye have not received the spirit of bondage again to fear" (Romans 8:15).

No more convincing testimony is on record than that of Job, how "the thing which he feared came upon him, and that which he was afraid of came unto him." Look what Job's fears reaped for him: defeat, depression, destruction, disease, and disaster.

The Bible commands; *"Neither give place to the devil"* (Ephesians 4:27). When you give place to fear, you are giving place to the devil.

Resist fear in Jesus's name. Plead the blood of Jesus against every fear. Quote the words of God aloud against diabolical fear!

5

FEAR ACTIVATES DISASTER IN YOUR HOME

It is crucial that we never give into the "fear that produces in kind" in our home and family life.

Fear produces bondage and bondage is always the result of Satan's workings. As a result, fear always activates Satan. It causes him to get busy bringing about the destruction and disaster that you fear. I have seen what fear can activate in my own family life.

In 1957, Joyce and I purchased our first home. It cost $11,000, and the payments were $79 per month. In today's standards, those amounts are next to nothing; but in the 1950s, with a very limited and uncertain income, $79 per month was quite an amount of money. I was traveling in evangelistic work. It was always a struggle to receive sufficient money to support my wife and five children. There were some weeks I was not engaged in special meetings. Consequently, there was no income during that week.

A battle in the realm of the spirit began. I began to fear that I would not be able to make those monthly payments. Each time I would turn on to the road where my family lived, an overwhelming fear would grip me that we would soon lose that home.

Fear activated Satan. While the circumstances cannot be explained in just black and white details, surely enough..."the thing which I greatly feared came upon me. That which I was afraid of came unto me." I reaped the results of my fears. We moved elsewhere to do the Lord's work. A friend put our house up for rent for us. The woman who rented it refused to pay the rent. A sheriff's order was acquired to try to evict her. The woman was extremely clever and was always gone when the sheriff's deputies came to deliver the eviction notice. We had no extra money to pay our house payment plus rent in the new city where we were living.

I'm confident my fears activated Satan to produce such a calamity. Satan must have had a gleeful time, causing this woman to avoid paying the rent, and causing us to have to return our home to the builder. It was a heartbreaking loss.

Then the Holy Spirit gave me the life-changing visitation in 1961. One of the affirmations He gave me was this one, *"Never again will I confess fear, for God hath not given me the spirit of fear; but of power, and of love, and of a sound mind"* (2 Timothy 1:7). With this new discipline to my spirit, Joyce and I began to take bold steps of faith. We made application to purchase another home. It was another battleground for me the day we signed the papers. Satan attempted to bring back the old tormenting fears that had beset me when we purchased our first home.

I knew if I gave place to fear, I would activate Satan to do his work of theft as he did in 1959. Jesus revealed Satan's sinister nature in John 10:10, *"The thief cometh not, but for to steal, and to kill, and to destroy: I am come that you might have life, and that more abundantly."* When one gives place to fear, you give place to the elements of Satan that are designed for destruction, theft, and death.

I must praise the Lord that after purchasing our home in 1961, we have never missed a single payment, nor have we ever been late. As I write these lines, that home is nearly paid for Satan has had no opportunity to steal this home from us, for I have steadfastly refused to give place to fear.

DO NOT FEAR A DISASTER IN YOUR MARRIAGE

As I write these lines, my wife, Joyce, and I have just celebrated 30 years of married life together. I am aware that in this day of high divorce rate and bitter marriages, it is an achievement for a couple to stay together 30 years. I'm grateful for God's help and mercy. There are certain principles of marriage that I wish to address today.

I have talked with many people who are married and to those whose marriages have failed. I have endeavored to discover the ingredients that make a marriage last and why marriages crumble. I am convinced that God wants us to experience abundant life in our marriages. This is far more than simply existing together in a bad arrangement.

Most marriages are severely tested. Husbands and wives do experience misunderstandings, suffering, pain and temptation, yet can rise above all of this and enjoy their lives together.

I believe good advice for marriage is this: "Don't put off until next year, or ten years from now the time to begin enjoying your marriage. Don't postpone working for a positive and constructive marriage until things will be 'ideal'." One man said, "I thought when I got out of my deep debts and the children were raised that our marriage would be happy. Now my debts are reduced and the children are all grown, but my wife and I still aren't happy." Yet another man said, "My wife and I looked forward to our retirement, then we would be able to enjoy each other more. But not so. I realize we let life pass us by and failed to enjoy living together as we went along."

Many look for some "Utopia type of life" when things will be better. But God's plan for us is to live now, for today, not for uncertain tomorrow. The Bible says, *"A merry heart doeth good like a medicine: but a broken spirit drieth the bones"* (Proverbs 17:22). That is, allow a merry heart to exist in your marriage. This joy of the Lord is your strength. Surely a joyful marriage should abound with the joy of the Lord, not just earthly happiness.

Like a personal Christian walk, when marriage loses its joy, it becomes weak and vulnerable to all kinds of problems and defeats. My wife and I enjoy going away alone at times, and those are pleasant, care-free times together. However, those experiences are the exception, not the rule. It's the day-by-day dwelling together joyfully that counts!

For any normal marriage, there are problems: sickness, unexpected trouble, financial difficulties, and confusion, even death. But life goes on day-by-day and it's a shame when couples don't really enjoy it together.

There was a time when I sadly observed the breakdown of a marriage that was close to me. It began when the husband started confiding in another woman about his problems. This lady was eager to console my friend. It seemed innocent enough at the start, but it opened the door to a secret affair: adultery.

No husband or wife should tell their marriage troubles to a third party. Especially not someone of the opposite sex who suddenly fills the role of intimate friend. Even your closest friend of the same sex doesn't need to know all the struggles of your marriage. When you confide in someone else, sooner or later you may discover that this third party has revealed your personal troubles to others and your testimony is damaged. Even if the Lord leads you to marriage counseling, it should be as husband and wife or with your spouse's permission.

We are commanded, *"Trust in the LORD with all thine, heart; lean not unto thine own understanding. In all thy ways acknowledge him, and he shall direct thy paths"* (Proverbs 3:5-6). We must lean on Jesus Christ in our times of testing, even in marriage problems. Blessed are the husbands and wives who learn not only to be marriage partners, but true friends!

Even though your marriage may have its share of pressures and intense disagreements, it doesn't mean that divorce is a solution. Remember how Job sadly declared, *"The thing which I greatly feared is come upon me, and that which I was afraid of is come unto me"* (Job 3:25). We should never entertain fear concerning our marriage

A lovely young wife, whose divorce was to be finalized within a week, confessed, I wish now I had never used the word *divorce.* We had been married only five years, but we argued so often. Things got pretty bad and one day I blurted out, "I think we ought to get a divorce."

"We were both shocked at first. We had never even thought of divorce before that moment, but after the shock wore off, I realized the seed had been planted. It was easier to say the next time. Within weeks that's all we talked about. The seed grew monstrous roots that finally strangled our marriage."

Others who have been divorced say the same thing. "Tell everybody you can," they say, "to never even speak the word *divorce*. There is something fatal in the very use of the word."

The Bible says, *"Death and life are in the power of the tongue: and they that love it shall eat the fruit thereof"* (Proverbs 18:21).

It's true that what you say is what you get. Unfortunately, this works for the bad as well as the good. There are certain words we must never utter as Bible believing Christians. *Divorce is* one of those words we must never employ. Ask most divorced persons; they will tell you that they began to talk divorce long before it became a reality.

This principle is also true: what you *fear* is what *you get*. Fear a divorce and you could be writing your own ticket for a divorce.

I think it's necessary to pause here and review some important things about making a marriage successful:

(1) Satan the foul thief who comes to steal, kill, and destroy is strongly arrayed against your marriage. It is his ultimate plan to cause your marriage to conclude by divorce. We must not be ignorant of his evil workings; we must resist him by first submitting unto God for His help and grace.

(2) We must not entertain in our hearts any fear of divorce. Fear has its origin in Satan; we must refuse to give place to fear, even the fear of a divorce. When fearful thoughts grip your mind that your marriage is headed for the rocks, employ your spiritual weapons which are mighty through God to the pulling down of Satan's strongholds.

The book of Proverbs is a powerful commentary on the power of words. A study of this book reveals not only the ability of right words to enable one to conquer life's problems, but also set forth are the destructive elements of the wrong kind of words. A worthwhile study is to go through Proverbs and mark those passages dealing with words, the mouth, the lips, and the tongue.

We must never speak those words that we don't want to become a part of our lives. Don't say such things as, "My wife and I are so unhappy," or "My husband is stupid."

One middle-aged wife said, "Somebody has to keep my husband humble. He gets so much attention from others he needs to be brought down a peg or two. He gets too big for his britches. I know just how to straighten him out." And that woman reaps the consequences of her words by sowing strife in her marriage.

Every husband needs a wife who will build him up, not tear him down. It's no sin to encourage each other with sincere compliments. Surely there are more good things in your partner than there are bad things.

A divorced woman said, "My husband's been gone for over three years now. How I wish he would come back. The loneliness is unbearable. There are a million things I forgot to tell him. If I had only let him know how good he really was, in so many ways. What a fool I was-I could never learn to compliment him; I was always on his back, pointing out all his mistakes. I see now how some husbands and wives treat each other so coldly, and I want to scream at them, 'Wake up, before it's too late! Quit your sarcasm, and encourage each other.'"

David Wilkerson wrote this about love and right words in a marriage: "Learn how to say, 'I'm sorrry!'—and mean it! Love, according to the Word of God, is learning how to say, 'I'm sorry.'

"An irate husband boasted, 'I walked out on my wife last night. She is always right, and I'm always wrong. But not this time. I'm not going to let her walk all over me Again. I know I'm right on this matter; I'm always the one who has to give in first. Well, this time I'm staying away until she crawls On her hands and knees and admits she's dead wrong.'

"Along with learning to say, 'I'm wrong,' husbands and wives must learn how to say 'I forgive.' Jesus warned the forgiveness of our Heavenly Father depends on our forgiving those who trespass against us.

Has your husband or wife cheated on you? Was there a true repentance? Are you trying hard to forgive? If he or she has shown evidence of godly sorrow and every effort is being made to make it up to you. You must forgive.

"And you must avoid bringing up the past. Multiplied thousands of marriages have survived infidelity, but only because godly sorrow for sin was followed by Christlike forgiveness."

Jesus Christ taught us clearly, "*And when ye stand praying forgive, if you have ought against any: that your Father also which is in heaven may forgive you your trespasses. But if ye do not forgive, neither will your Father which is in heaven forgive your trespasses*" (Mark 11:25-26).

Again the Bible commands, "*The discretion of a man deferreth his anger; and it is his glory to pass over a transgression*" (Proverbs 19:11).

God is very much interested in helping our marriages. He gave the blueprint in His Word; it's up to us to trust His grace to enable us to achieve success. Satan is viciously opposed to our marriage success. He sows seeds of fear, wrong speaking, defeatist attitudes to rob us of all that is, good and designed for our happiness. Give no place to Fear...even the fear of divorce and its subsequent miseries.

6

THE FEAR OF CRITICISM

He was in the public's eye. His name was a byword around the world. He was denounced as a hypocrite, an imposter, and a murderer. A newspaper cartoon depicted him on a guillotine with a big knife raised to sever his head. Crowds jeered at him, hissed at him as he rode through the streets. He probably was one of the most criticized men of his day. Who was he? His name was George Washington the first President of the United States, and one of the most revered leaders of any nation.

Whenever anyone endeavors to do something, just anything, he may rest assured that he will be criticized. This is very true, even in the ranks of Christians. Criticism is usually a defense mechanism utilized to bolster one's ego or to give a sense of self-esteem by lowering the self-esteem of someone else. Chronic fault-finding, belittling the other fellow and nagging are all symptoms of low self-esteem. As someone has well said, "You have to be little to belittle." In order to escape the conviction in one's own heart for spiritual laziness, people criticize the active one for doing a job.

I discovered a long time ago that, as a radio minister, there's absolutely nothing I can do to avoid some kinds of criticism, I minister to people in all walks of life and with varying levels of intelligence. What appeals to one does not appeal to the other. If you will examine the letters to the editor column of any magazine or newspaper, one man after reading a certain article will say, "Cancel my subscription." But someone else will say, "That's the best article on the subject I've ever read." So let's face it, we're going to be criticized. Criticized if we do and criticized if we don't.

Dale Carnegie once said, "No one ever kicked a dead dog. The more lively the dog, the more pleasure people get out of kicking him." Jesus traveled with twelve disciples. They became His most intimate friends, but one of the twelve tamed traitor to Him and another openly deserted Him the moment He got in serious trouble. Thus, two out of twelve gave Him trouble. Why should you or I expect to do any better?

The Bible indicates that there was not a greater man in all Israel than Moses, and yet we read over and over again in the Word, "And the people murmured against Moses."

We cannot avoid criticism. As long as we keep active for God, seeking to extend His Kingdom, people will continue to criticize us.

If criticism cannot be avoided, we must learn how to handle it. Of course, some criticism is just, and we should take it to heart and let it help us. Every time I receive a critical letter in the mail, I carefully analyze that letter to see if the contents are true. If anything said is true, I try to examine myself and see how to improve on that area my critic has faulted.

But I am particularly concerned with the unjust criticism that we as Christian receive.

We should realize that we cannot spend our time trying to pacify those who criticize. By trying to fix it up with one person, we usually get in wrong with someone else. Our task as Christians, however, is to please God and do what God wants us to do. If we are certain that we have done that, then we must close out mind to the criticism, ignore it completely. We must make up our mind that we would rather hear the Master's "well done" than win the favor of all the people. In most cases, it's impossible to please the people entirely and to please our God, too.

Let us seek to please God, to do what God wants us to do in the task for which He has called us. Let people criticize if they must.

I am reminded of as story I read a long time ago. At a railroad station on a rainy day, the gatekeeper made everyone stop before going on the platform, put down their suitcases on the wet pavement and, while standing in the rain, show their ticket. Of each in turn, the gatekeeper insisted that this be done. People were angry. They called the gatekeeper various names. Stone-faced, he ignored the barbs completely and insisted on seeing each ticket.

Finally, one man near the end of the line said to him, "You're not very popular around here are you?"

The gatekeeper replied, "No, not around here, but my boss told me just the other day that I will soon get a promotion because I was the best gatekeeper of the railroad company."

In the same way, we sometimes find that in carrying out the King's orders we cannot gain the favor of all the people nor keep them happy. We must continue to endeavor in all things to gain the favor and smile of approval of our Lord Jesus Christ. He knows what is best.

Let's do our God-given duties as we see them. The God we trust with our soul is well, able to take care of our reputation.

CRITICAL LETTERS

Quite often I receive letters in the mail that are critical and unkind toward this ministry of world evangelism. I received this letter from a man who listens to my broadcast:

"I've been promising for a year and a half to write you a letter. I found out by your preaching that you don't know anything, and all you can do is preach to the Indians in the north, and to the blacks in the south. And now you're going to the West Indies. Why don't you stay at home: that's where you belong. No one asked you to go there to the West Indies.

"You call the people down there heathen, but they are more God-fearing than you are. You have no right to call civilized people heathen. They can get along without anyone like you. All you're going down there for is to grab money, that's all you are is a money grabber, a liar and a hypocrite."

It was John Wesley who used to tell his young preachers, "Unless you get someone saved, or someone mad, you're not even called to preach!" By John Wesley's qualifications, perhaps I am called to preach. For by the power of the Spirit of God, we are getting souls saved, and others get mad by my preaching, as evidenced by this letter.

I do thank God we are being used of Him to stir hearts through our broadcast. Many to great blessings, others who angrily reject the message.

I want to make a few observations about this letter:

You don't know anything, and all you can do is preach to the Indians in the north, and to the blacks in the south. And now you're going to the West Indies.

It's true. I have gone repeatedly to preach to the Indians and blacks. Hundreds of times I've preached to them. And the Lord has rewarded our ministry by giving us thousands of precious souls who have received Jesus Christ as their personal Savior. I call it a sacred privilege to preach to these dear people.

No one asked you to go to the I West Indies, Why don't you stay at home?

The truth is that I've received many urgent letters from various islands of the West Indies, urging me to come for gospel ministry. However, if no one at all had asked me to come, I'm still obligated to go. For Jesus said in the Great Commission, *"Go ye into all the world, and preach the gospel to every creature"* (Mark 16:15). I am going because Jesus commanded me to go.

You have no right to call civilized people heathen.

In the biblical evaluation, every person without Jesus Christ as personal Savior is a heathen soul, whether he lives in a mansion or a jungle hut. Yes, every person without Christ is heathen, spiritually dead in trespasses and sins (see Ephesians 2:1), having complete darkness of soul.

All you're going to the West Indies for is to grab money.

The facts are the people of the West Indies are quite poor, with a per capita income much less than people in Canada and the United States. If my objective were to grab money, that's about the last place to go! God knows, however, that I do not go there, for money. I go for gospel ministry, open air crusades, television crusades, and personal ministry to influence all the people we can with the gospel for everlasting life.

The man said in opening his letter that, "You *don't know anything.*"

I wish to kindly take exception to that statement, for here are some things I know for sure:

"I know whom I have believed, and am persuaded that he is able to keep that which I have committed unto him against that day" (2 Timothy 1:12).

"I know that all things work together for good to them that love God, to them who are called according to his purpose" (Romans 8:28).

"I know that my redeemer liveth" (Job 19:25).

"I know that [my Lord] *canst do every thing"* (Job 42:2).

With Jesus, *"I speak that which I do know"* (John 3:11).

And I know this wonderful Christ. This is far more than just knowing about Him. I know Him as a real, divine Person who is with me as I go to the West Indies, or anywhere else in His name!

"And hereby do we know that we know Him" (1 John 2:3).

FEAR OF CRITICISM

You will never witness for Christ with effectiveness, you will never minister healing to the sick, and you will never be God's instrument to cast out devils, as long as you are shackled by the fear of criticism.

Those who have this fear of criticism are *self-conscious.* In testimony they are nervous, timid, ill-at-ease. This inferiority complex is not of God. "Ye are in Christ' and "Christ is in you" are two of the most wonderful statements of the Bible. When you are in Christ, and Christ is in you, then your life is Christ-controlled, and there is nothing inferior about Christ.

If you go on ruled by this fear of criticism, you will know torment abundant, and you will live just as the Bible describes, *"The fear of man bringeth a snare: but whoso putteth his trust in the* Lord *shall be safe"* (Proverbs 29:25).

What are the results? Failure in your undertakings. Lack of confidence in your capable witness for Christ, hesitancy in warfare, reluctance to step out boldly to be used God.

7

ALIBIS AND EXCUSES

Of late I've been called upon to counsel with different men who desire to do the Lord's work but are hindered from doing so because of a long list of excuses. Some of them are "*justifiable*" but most of them are restricted by that little word *if*.

Years ago I read a statement by E. W. Kenyon, "Don't say what you would do IF circumstances were right. Wipe out that IF and go on and conquer."

For years of my ministry, I worked under the secure wing of a large ministry or organization. With William Freeman, then T. L. Osborn, then with the largest organization in the world in Full Gospel circles, I was somewhat sheltered.

But in 1961, when God led us to pioneer our ministry across Canada, by radio, literature and crusading, there were dozens of "ifs" that would have defeated us before we began, had we allowed them to do so.

"IF we had enough money, we could undertake this radio and publication ministry …"

How that big IF about money stared us in the face! When we decided to return to Canada and turn our backs upon golden opportunities that existed for us elsewhere, we had no money at all. In fact, I had to borrow $75 from my mother to return to Canada.

But God was leading us step by step. It was rigorous testing. The going got tougher before it got better. But we had come to the kingdom for such an hour as this.

We signed radio contracts with no funds at all; simply believing the Lord would see us through. Unreasonable? Surely, but that's the blessed life of faith.

When people confront me with this negative statement, "If I only had enough money, I would step out for God," I share with them our testimony, and how the same God will respond to meet their needs, IF only they will have rugged faith in God and His Word!

IF I didn't have a wife and family, what all I could do for the Lord...

How often I've heard this remark by sincere men. I've known men who, sulk and balk and make their whole family miserable, because they have a wife and children.

One would-be minister said that to me a short time ago, trying to give an excuse for not doing what he felt was the Lord's will for his life.

I said, "Look, man, let's be honest and face up to this matter. You fathered your children and it is your job to raise them. You must meet this God-given responsibility first, before you try to set the world on fire."

IF I could live my life over again, how differently I would do things...

Now, this is an honest statement, denoting a quality of good thinking. However, too often it is an evasion to keep from doing what needs to be done. As long as you are here on this earth, *now* is your opportunity to make your life count for God and for good. Living in hopeless regrets is vain, and futile.

Have you failed thus far in attaining your true purpose in life? Then determine to start how, to live life at your best for the glory of God.

"Whether therefore ye eat, or drink, or whatsoever ye do, do all to the glory of God" (I Corinthians 10:31).

IF only I were younger, then I could plan my life better...

This age complex is one of the biggest excuses people make to bind their effectiveness. Almost everyone I meet is either "too young" or "too old." Nonsense! Be optimistic about your present age.

E. W. Kenyon, a man whose ministry and writings I greatly admire, didn't start writing until he was 57 years of age. He wrote three of his most treasured books, *In His Presence, The Hidden Man,* and *The Blood Covenant* when he was nearly 80 years old.

Refuse to be caught in that deceitful web of "age bondage," whether young or old. Be useful to God at your present age, whatever it is.

IF I were more sure of myself, I could likely succeed...

This message of boldness in the Lord means confidence, courage, fearlessness and daring. Your confidence, of course, is not in the flesh but in Christ Jesus, declares the Apostle Paul.

However, the Lord does instill within us a healthy confidence that we can, by His grace, do whatever He wants done. *"I can do all things through Christ which strengtheneth me"* (Philippians 4:13). *"Not that we are sufficient of ourselves to think anything as of ourselves; but our sufficiency is of God"* (2 Corinthians 3:5).

Wipe out that IF and go on in the ability the Lord gives you!

IF I had a good education, then I would be ready to do the Lord's work...

Certainly education is important in this present generation in almost all facets of life. All of us, I'm sure, desire more education.

However, many successful ministers and gospel workers have, sincerely given their limited education to God, and the Lord has been pleased to use them in His vineyard.

A world-renowned evangelist whom I know well had a very limited education. Yet, he became a student in the highest sense, in that he has never ceased to educate himself in varied fields, until today he is not only a top evangelist but also is admired by highly educated men for his "genius."

IF I had the talent some have for speaking, I know I could make it...

This is such a prominent alibi among Christians! However, God has blessed us with the physical ability to speak. Therefore, no matter how great or small that ability is, the Lord can use it for His glory.

Remember how those who knew me well were so dubious about my entering the ministry, because I always had such difficulty in speaking, especially publicly.

In high school, I was elected president of my student body. One teacher said to me privately one day, "Don, you are a good boy, and everyone likes you. But it is a pity you have never learned to speak publicly!" He was referring to my stumbling attempts to lead the student assemblies. I was a failure.

But two Bible promises gave me the strength I needed to overcome, and through the help of the Spirit, I learned to speak effectively. *"Now therefore go, and I will be with thy mouth, and teach thee what thou shalt say"* (Exodus 4:12). And again the testimony of David, *"The Spirit of the LORD spake by me, and His word was in my tongue"* (2 Samuel 23:2).

By accepting these two verses to help with my inability to speak, I conquered this terrific speech handicap, and by God's help have preached nearly 6,000 public sermons, and thousands of radio messages.

"It is not by might, nor by power, but by my Spirit, saith the LORD of hosts" (Zechariah 4:6).

IF I had good health, then I could do the Lord's work...

It is not an unrealistic statement to affirm that the same Lord who wants you to do His work will also provide you with health for the task!

If you really want to overcome your health problems, then do these things: (1) Quit talking about your health to others; it never helps you to talk to others about your bad health. All you can hope to gain is sympathy and pity, and that will never produce the health you so need. (2) Quit worrying about your health. Worry never solved a problem, healed a sickness, or paid a bill. And worry hasn't helped you, as you well know.

I boldly affirm that God heals His servants and desires to bless them with good healthy bodies and strong minds!

IF I could only get the right breaks, I know I could go...

Getting breaks is not the secret of success in the Lord's work. Favor cometh from the Lord. God may often use others to encourage you, but don't be deluded into waiting for "breaks." Rather, make your "breaks."

IF nothing happens to stop me, I will make it...

Better confess this fact, *"If God be for us, who can be against us?"* (Romans 8:3 1). For the dedicated gospel laborer, actually *nothing* can stop you, for nothing can stop the God who dwells within you, to empower you.

This is really a flimsy alibi that is a sure forerunner of failure. Whatever "things" attempt to block your progress, boldly affirm this truth, *"Nay, in all these things we are more than conquerors through Christ"* (Romans 8:37).

IF television hadn't come in and taken over, I could do it...

Television has been blamed for many of the present day evils and ills, and rightly so. However, the invasion of TV as an alibi, or reason for failure is not sound.

I must admit that I once allowed this IF about the impact of TV to hinder me from doing the Lord's will about my radio ministry.

The Lord had shown me the limitless possibilities of gospel broadcasting way back in 1951 when I was just 21 years old, I knew then that the Lord called me to be a radio minister. For the next six years I was. Then I got the idea that nobody listened to radio, that TV had taken over. Consequently, I abandoned my radio ministry for a time.

One vital lesson I learned was this: when God calls, He doesn't tolerate circumstances to overrule His divine call.

So in 1961, I re-entered the ministry of gospel broadcasting full-time every day. To my amazement, I read that millions more radios were in use than ever before! Also, I discovered that around the world radio was increasingly popular.

Hence, wiping out the miserable "IF," I began to take steps to place our broadcasts on outreaches around the world into 89 nations. What a reception, we have had! The Lord has made our broadcasts a means of soul-saving, healing and deliverance to multitudes all over the world... by radio.

IF I could move to a new place, and get a new start...

Sometimes that may help. But the Bible truth is...the Lord wants you to begin *doing* His will right where you are. Not waiting for a new place, but there where you are. "Be my witness first in Jerusalem."

"Go home to thy friends, and tell them what great things the Lord hath done for thee, and hath had compassion on thee" (Mark 5:19).

IF I had the personality of some people I know...

The Lord will use you and make you a blessing, not because of your dynamic personality, but because of your dedication to Him.

"The Lord looketh not on the outward appearance, but upon the heart." The Lord sees your heart and will use you, as your heart is clean, pure, anointed and yielded to Him.

It is not wrong to seek to correct the personality defects that are a drawback. Ask your spouse, or someone close to you, to help you with these. But in the final analysis, it is "the hidden man of the heart " cultivated by the Word and the Spirit that makes you effective for God.

IF only I didn't have the 'past' that I do, I could do the Lords work…

When you read the Bible, you fully realize that God is so merciful, longsuffering and ready to forgive. This does not mean you can trifle with Him and seek to take advantage of "easy-for-givism," as someone called it.

One young minister told me, "When it comes to matters of money, I would rather repent than pay." I clarified this fellow's way of thinking, to instill within him a holy fear of God.

On the other hand, God will forgive your past and give you a new start. The Lord gave a new start to David, Jonah, Peter, and Mark, among others.

God specializes in *restoration,* when one sincerely repents and turns from his past sinning. In spite of your guilty past, God can and will use you again.

IF I hadn't failed once before, I would have the heart to try again...

Your memory is your worst enemy. This attitude is fatal to success. Of course, this fear of failure is the tool of the devil to club you for life. Anyone who has ever achieved anything for God has met with failures, discouragements, and overwhelming setbacks. But as a bold, Bible living Christian, you must be persistent, violent, undenying, wholehearted...and as sure as the sun rises each morning, you shall succeed!

I'm sure you have seen yourself in some of these fatal "IFs." There is an awful price to pay for using these alibis, and that price is failure, lack of fulfillment, missing God's best.

Remember: You must "Wipe out the IF and go on and conquer!"

8

THE CHALLENGE OF FEAR

When Dr. Graham told me how my little daughter, Jeanne Michelle, was born with afflicted feet and hands and a severe restriction of her respiratory system, the devil began to visit me with thoughts that she would never live to be a grown girl. I battled these spirits of fear repeatedly for the next several years in our faith fight for Jeanne's life and health.

On her seventh birthday in 1960, we went to visit my wife's parents. Grandpa Shackelford said to me, "Don, I think there's something seriously wrong with Jeanne. It appears to me that she might have tuberculosis or some other critical lung disease."

"No, I think Jeanne is all right," I replied. "She's thin and not as active as her brothers and sisters, but she's all right," I tried to assure him and myself. Again Grandpa warned me, I wish you'd take her, for a complete examination to see what is wrong. I don't like the symptoms that I see, and I think a doctor's examination is in order."

So we took Jeanne back to Dr. Graham and he made thorough tests, using X-rays and a fluoroscope. The doctor confirmed Grandpa's concern. Jeanne was indeed stricken with a critical lung disease, the severity of which they could not determine immediately. Further tests were made which verified that she was critically ill.

The spirits of fear that I battled in the days and nights ahead were tremendous. In this spiritual warfare, I received a biblical understanding that fear does not originate from God. Fear is Satan's gift to us. I made a decision to refuse these spirits of fear. In Jesus's name I resisted them and received God's bountiful gifts of power, love and a sound mind.

In our evangelistic travels that took us from Tulsa to Chicago, then on to Vancouver, British Columbia, we were holding our hearts steady for a complete liberation for Jeanne.

One day in Chicago, A. T. Smith, a beloved African-American brother, stopped in the midst of a park and said, "Brother Gossett, I believe now is the time for us to take deliverance for little Jeanne. Let's lay hands on her and cast out the spirits of infirmity and receive the Lord's healing for her."

We all stopped, right in the middle of this park in downtown Chicago, and had a beautiful prayer session in behalf of Jeanne. We were thoroughly convinced that the Lord, by His Spirit, had done the work fully for Jeanne at that moment!

Later tests by Dr. Graham and other physicians confirmed what the Lord Jesus had done: Jeanne was completely healed of the critical lung disease. Praise the Lord!

A few times through the years, Satan sought to inflict me with that spirit of fear concerning an untimely death for Jeanne, but I had learned to resist him and had deliverance from this diabolical fear for good. Today, Jeanne is married and the mother of my two beautiful grandchildren! The Lord is faithful to His Word!

THE CHALLENGE OF FEAR

We must have a rebellion against the adversary of fear. We cannot be namby-pamby, non-resistant, passive individuals who allow Satan to trample over us by his threatening tread.

First Samuel 17 is one of the most interesting stories of the Bible. The Philistines stood on a mountain on one side and Israel, stood on a mountain on the other side and there was a valley between them, the Scripture declares. I have been to this valley of Elah and in my mind could visualize the battle scene.

The champion of the Philistines, Goliath, a towering giant, threw down a challenge to the men of Israel to come and fight with him. "I defy the armies of Israel this day; give me a man, that we may fight together."

"When Saul and all Israel heard the words of the Philistine, they were dismayed, and greatly afraid."

Later, when David came to the army camp, he, too, heard the words of Goliath. He witnessed this reaction, "And all the men of Israel, when they saw the man, fled from him, and were sore afraid."

When David protested Goliath's challenge, Eliab, David's eldest brother, ridiculed him. But David was not discouraged. He countered with these words, "What have I now done? Is there not a cause?" David represented the Lord's cause for deliverance in this circumstance and he was not dismayed. He was ready to be the Lord's instrument to "take away the reproach from Israel" (verse 26).

So it was that David continued to speak from one person to the other affirming his bold confidence in God's ability to triumph over Goliath. Finally, his words were repeated before King Saul, and he sent for David. David assured the king, "Let no man's heart fail because of him; thy servant will go and fight with this Philistine."

However, King Saul was not impressed by David's physical appearance nor did he think he had any chance of conquest in battle with Goliath.

THE POWER OF TESTIMONY

David had a glorious testimony, and he was quick to share it: While caring for his father's sheep, he was opposed by a lion and then a bear. Through the ability given him by God, he conquered both the lion and the bear, and this uncircumcised Philistine would be even as one of these wild beasts, "seeing he has defied the armies of the living God," declared David.

David was not confident in his own strength but in the might of the Lord: "The Lord that delivered me out of the paw of the lion, and out of the paw of the bear, He will deliver me out of the hand of this Philistine."

The Philistine Goliath also disdained David and tried to ridicule him. However, David waxed bold and said unto him, "Thou comest to me with a sword, and with a spear, and with a shield: but I come to thee in the name of the Lord of Hosts, the God of the armies of Israel whom thou hast defied."

One impressive lesson about the account in 1 Samuel 17 is this: David did not look like a conqueror, but he talked like one! If negative, pessimistic people could have discouraged David, he would have been well discouraged. First, he was ridiculed by his oldest brother telling him that it was pride and the haughtiness of his heart that caused him to come down to see the so-called battle. Then King Saul said to him, "You are not able to go against this Philistine to fight with him: for you are but a youth, and he a man of war from his youth." Goliath disdained him with these words, "Am I a dog, that thou comest to me with staves? And the Philistine cursed David by his gods."

But David's attitude concerning this fearful circumstance was this, "For who is this uncircumcised Philistine, that he should defy the armies of the living God?" David was indignant that spirits of fear would reduce God's men to such a display of cowardice. And so it is, if we are to overcome the challenge of fear today, we must be defiant.

Further, Goliath continued his verbal assault against David, "Come to me, and I will give thy flesh unto the fowls of the air, and to the beasts of the field."

In the eyes of Eliab, King Saul, and Goliath, David didn't look like a conqueror. But he knew, by God's grace and ability, he was more than a conqueror, and he talked like one.

To conquer fear, we must be bold in our confession of God's ability. We must say what God says about the subject of fear. We must agree with God and disagree with the devil.

NOT WORDS ONLY BUT ACTION

After all of David's bold words to those who would oppose him, he was a man not only of words, but a man of action. Our confession of faith precedes our possession of victory. Our words precede our action. As a matter of fact, words motivate and stimulate to daring action.

So when it came time for action, David hastened and ran toward the Philistine. In his heart he knew the Lord would give him conquest. By his confession, he declared what would be the outcome. Then, by his actions, he arose to the situation with confidence.

By his smooth stone, he felled the giant and then, by the giant's own sword, cut his head off.

Because David was God's instrument to overcome fear, it was not the Israelites who fled but it was the Philistines.

David's victory ignited the hearts of the men of Israel to arise, "and shout and pursue the Philistines."

There is deliverance from fear, and no one in the Bible practiced a life of overcoming the challenge of fear more remarkably than did David!

9

THE WEAPONS OF OUR WARFARE

T*he weapons of our warfare are not carnal, but mighty through God to the pulling down of strongholds"* (2 Corinthians 10:4).

Fear is no light thing to those experiencing it. Satan uses the spirit of fear and masquerades it in the form of more acceptable words such as doubt, anxiety, indecision and alarm. But from there, fear takes on monstrous proportions.

However, the Bible says that we are not to be ignorant of Satan's devices, for the weapons of our warfare are not carnal, but mighty through God to the pulling down of the devil's strongholds.

There are several weapons that we will discuss here. But there is one outstanding weapon that stands above all others in fighting the enemy of fear. The weapon that can totally, permanently conquer fear is a rugged, daring faith in God's Word. *"Taking the shield of faith, wherewith you shall be able to quench all the fiery darts of the wicked"* (Ephesians 6:16). Faith based on God's Word is indestructible and irresistible.

THE WORD. GOD'S INVINCIBLE WEAPON

I want to show you God's invincible weapon of the Word, which is so "quick and powerful." I want you to see that for every form of fear forged by satanic ingenuity, God has an answer in His Word. Believe what God says, agree with His Word to you, and you can start on the road of deliverance from fear.

Do you fear being incapable? The "I canters" are a multitude. They speak like this, "I can't witness for Christ. I can't live an overcoming life. I can't sleep at night. I can't pay my bills." On and on they profess their inabilities. How do you overcome the fear of being incapable? By the affirmation of Philippians 4:13: *"I can do all things through Christ which strengtheneth me."* Whatever the Lord wants you to do, He will give you the ability and strength to do it.

Does the Lord want you to write a letter to someone concerning his salvation? Then the Lord gives you the ability to write that letter with effectiveness, permeated with the convicting power of the Holy Spirit.

Does the Lord want you to minister to someone who is sick? Then the Lord has equipped you with divine ability to lay your believing hands upon that sick person and expect positive results in Jesus's name.

Is the Lord leading you to minister deliverance to the one under demon control? Then, by supernatural endowment, you can speak the words of deliverance in Jesus's mighty name!

Do you fear weakness? God promises you strength every day. Affirm it *"The* LORD *is the strength of my life; of whom shall I be afraid?"* (Psalm 27:1). Speak it boldly, *"The joy of the* LORD *is my strength"* (Nehemiah 8:10). Right now, be as Paul commanded the Ephesian believers, *"Be strong in the Lord, and in the power of his might"* (Ephesians 6:10).

And here is an exercise to overcome the fear of weakness:

SAY WHAT GOD COMMANDS YOU TO SAY:

"Let the weak say, I am strong" (Joel 3:10) *I am strong!*

No matter what I think of myself, *I am strong!*

Regardless of others, *I am strong!*

When I feel the weakest, *I am strong!*

In spite of past experiences, *I am strong!*

It is not when I am strong only that I say, *I am strong!*

But when I am weak, I am to say, *I am strong!*

God commands me to say, *I am strong!*

Wherever I am, *I am strong!*

Whatever I am, *I am strong!*

Whoever I am, *I am strong!*

This is the language of faith.

Do you fear insecurity? The fear of insecurity is one of Satan's subtle devices against Christians. He plagues young fathers with the fear of insecurity about providing for their families. He disturbs aged Christians with a fear of insecurity in their advanced years of life. He injects a fear of insecurity in the hearts of those who are in debt, plaguing them with thoughts of deeper debt and more insecurity. How can you be released from this fear of insecurity? By believing the Bible! By speaking God's Word! *"My God shall supply all your need according to His riches in glory by Christ Jesus"* (Philippians 4:19).

Here is an exercise in overcoming the fear of insecurity by the application of God's Word:

FINANCIAL SECURITY AND SUCCESS ARE CERTAIN...WHEN YOU: "LET THE WORD OF GOD PREVAIL" ACTS 19:20

No matter how many unpaid bills I have, *my God shall supply all my need!*

Regardless of how the economy is, *my God shall supply all my need!*

In spite of my bank account, *my God shall supply all my need!*

When financial embarrassment stares me in the face, *my God shall supply all my need!*

Regardless of the tight money situation, *my God shall supply all my need!*

In spite of past financial failures, *my God shall supply all my need!*

When things appear all wrong, *my God shall supply all my need!*

When things appear all right, *my God shall supply all my need!*

Wherever I am, *my God shall supply all my need!*

Whoever I am, *my God shall supply all my need!*

"My God shall supply all I need!"

Do you fear sickness and disease? This is one of the most prominent fears that vex countless individuals. Yet, the express will of God tells us in Acts 10:38, *"God anointed Jesus of Nazareth with the Holy Ghost and with power: who went about doing good, and healing all that were oppressed of the devil."* This very same Jesus is still healing all oppressed of the devil through His body today. *"Himself took out infirmities, and bare our sicknesses"* (Matthew 8:17). When you actually believe in your heart of hearts that

Jesus took your infirmities upon His own body and bare your sicknesses away by His provision, you will have no fear of sickness and disease. *"With his stripes we are healed"* (Isaiah 53:5). Jesus came to take off of us what the devil put on us. David testified of the Lord, *"Who forgiveth all thine iniquities; who healeth all thy diseases"* (Psalm 103:3).

Do you fear death? Outside of Jesus Christ, death certainly is an enemy to be feared. The Bible says, *"Jesus likewise took part of flesh and blood; that through death He might destroy him that had the power of death, that is the devil; and deliver them who through fear of death were all their lifetime subject to bondage"* (Hebrews 2:14-15). Jesus brings you a glorious announcement: *"I am the resurrection, and the life and whosoever liveth and believeth in me shall never die"* (John 11:25-26).

History tells us of a time when the Armenians were overrun by hostile, heathen people. There were many Christians in Armenia, and they suffered great persecutions and slaughter.

One day, forty Armenian Christians were led out in line to be executed. They were given a choice: if they would deny Jesus Christ, they would be spared. One by one, they were led out into the circle and asked if they would deny Christ; everyone said, "No," and was shot...everyone but one. When they came to the last man and asked him if he would deny Christ, he said, "Yes," and was spared. The man who held the gun and did the shooting walked up to this last man, handed him the gun and said, "You take my place, and I will take yours."

The fortieth man took the gun and walked out to do the shooting. The soldier stood in the circle to be shot. He spoke, "First, let me speak; I want to tell you why I did this.

"I have stood out there and shot thirty-nine men, and every time I shot one, a beautiful white Angel came down and put a crown on his head. I saw the fortieth Angel coming with a crown, but the fortieth man was afraid and denied Christ. I want that crown; the Angel is here. You can shoot me, for I accept Christ and the crown."

"Be thou faithful unto death, and I will give thee a crown of life" (Revelation 2:10).

Do you fear evil? That evil that comes with the frightening tread of the giant Goliath. No one can ignore the evil that glowers, but we must not fear it. In Christ Jesus we have divine authority to battle against all evil. Go to the 91st Psalm that tells you of the blessed abiding place in the Lord where no plague shall come nigh your dwelling and no evil befall you. A German physician has said that the 91st Psalm is the best preservative in times of disease and cholera, and that its truth is heavenly medicine against plague and Pestilence. This 91st Psalm reveals the Eternal Protector with divine dominion over all evil. The supernatural army of God's heaven surrounds those who put their trust in God's Son.

And then, in the beloved 23rd Psalm, you can say with David, "I will fear no evil, for Thou art with me." What strength and courage you draw from these words! It reminds me of a stanza from a hymn which says:

I've seen the lightning flashing, and heard the thunder roll,
I've felt sin's breakers dashing, I trying to conquer my soul;
I've heard the voice of my Savior, telling me still to fight on;
He promised never to leave me, never to leave me alone.

In the light of God's Word you do not have to go on being the victim of fear. Get into the Word of God and let it get into you.

Satan cannot resist the Word of God. It was the Word, which Jesus so effectively used, when severely tempted of the devil. The Word says, *"Greater is he that is you, than he that is in the world"* (I John 4:4). Fear is of Satan. Power, love, soundness of mind, strength, and fearlessness are of God. Say with David, *"I sought the LORD, and he heard me, and delivered me from all my fears"* (Psalm 34:4).

ANOTHER POWERFUL WEAPON AGAINST FEARFUL LIVING

I have often related how early in my Christian life I was plagued by many different kinds of fear. I must also confess that during that time I did not have a powerful dimension of life to make me bold in the Spirit.

As I read the Word daily, I was already learning the importance of bold Bible living. But then came the day when I came face to face with the proposition: *Have I been filled with the Spirit?*

Now I knew it was the work of the Holy Spirit to produce salvation, to regenerate my spirit. But had I been filled with the Spirit? Some of my ministerial colleagues advised I had; others said, "No." I determined to read the Bible and discover for myself.

This led to a new study of the Word and the great passages in the book of Acts that told of the Holy Spirit coming on the day of Pentecost, at the house of Cornelius, and to the brethren at Ephesus. I was convinced that I could be filled with the Spirit, too. And it seemed important that I receive no less than the disciples, the mother of Jesus, and many others received. I praise

God that, while continuing on in my quest for God's best and for spiritual enabling, the Lord filled me with the Holy Spirit, and I began to speak with other tongues as the Spirit gave utterance!

This was a vital turning point in breaking from the old timidity; fear and reluctance that had held me back. The dynamic infilling of the Holy Ghost is something every believer, whether you are a preacher or not, should receive. I'm not advocating a theological debate as to the good of speaking in other tongues. I am challenging you to consider the way the early church ministered in boldness, in power, in effectiveness. If God is no respecter of persons, then we can have what they had.

Consider Peter: the fearful, cowardly Peter has stood just days before in the presence of Christ-hating people at the trail of Jesus, denied that he even knew the Lord and cursed to prove it. But now here he is on the day of Pentecost, clothed with an unexplainable power and able to preach a message that brought 3,000 converts into the church that one day! The Baptism in the Holy Spirit is truly a powerful weapon against fearful living.

MORE WEAPONS FOR YOUR SPIRITUAL ARSENAL

Here are some other offensive weapons against fear from a dear brother in the Lord, Fred Greve:

1. *If you are afraid, seek the Savior.* It is not true that no Christian ever fears; it is true that a Christian does not have to face his fears alone. He has a Savior. Redeemed people have a Person, not a theory. If, therefore, you are not a Christian, you should seek Jesus as your Savior now. The fear of the eternal results of sin is settled when Jesus is your personal Savior.

2. *If you are afraid, pray.* The disciples cried loudly from their ship, "Lord, save us: we perish." Not All such prayers are loud, but they all have a desperate quality. Instead of trying to conquer fear by willpower or by self-discipline alone, we must cry out desperately. Some might think it fashionable to talk about their worries, to tolerate them, but actually it is infinitely better to get rid of them.

3. *If you are afraid, sing.* Paul and Silas, not knowing what might befall them, sang praises in their prison cell. This is not whistling-in-the-dark self-assurance. It is the appropriation of God's help. Paul and Silas received that help and were miraculously released from prison. King Jehoshaphat of Judah also received help when he faced three large armies with joyful praises. The Bible tells us the story, *"And when they* [Judah] *began to sing and praise, the* LORD *set an ambush against them who were come against Judah and they* [Judah's enemies] *were smitten"* (2 Chronicles 20:22). We can find it possible to sing away our fears, too.

4. *If you are afraid, read the Bible.* The Bible is not magic; but it is Truth. Through the centuries, millions have received assurance through its statements. It is helpful to realize that men of the Bible had problems, too. They had fears and failures. These men of faith were not men insulated from fear; they were men who conquered fear. It is not unusual to experience fear, but it is a tragedy—if we do not rid ourselves of it by appropriating God's provision for us.

5. *If you are afraid serve.* No one has ever proved that we have a one-track mind. But practical experience has shown that if we occupy ourselves with good things, evil things must vanish. There is no greater cure for our personal fears than to help others in need. Victorious saints of God are persons who, though human and prone to fear, spend themselves in service and thus have no time for worry. Self-pity and fear are close twins.

6. If *you are afraid, trust.* Trust is a strong word. It means abandonment to God. Trust is not passive; it is very active. Implicit trust affirms God's truth. It does not say, "I wish the Lord would help me." It says, "The Lord is helping me now." If you are bothered by fear, repeat these Bible statements: "The Lord is my helper." "The Lord is with me." The promises, of God are couched in positive language. *"For all the promises of God in him are yea, and in him amen"* (2 Corinthians 1:20).

In the midst of today's tensions—caused by the sin in the world—the true believer looks to Jesus, knowing that his redemption is at hand.

10

OVERCOMING THE FEAR OF FAILURE

I'm on the Island of Antigua in the West Indies as I write this chapter. It was years ago, in Antigua, that my wife, Joyce, and I experienced one of our most serious setbacks in the ministry. In early 1964, the Lord of the harvest nudged our hearts that we should lift up our eyes and behold the ripened harvest fields of this world. For the first fifteen years of our ministry, we had devoted out entire attention to ministry across Canada and the United States.

We had launched a radio ministry in the West Indies on a station in Puerto Rico. Invitations came for missionary crusades.

Joyce and I felt quite noble, almost heroic, as we boarded an Air Canada jet to fly away to the West Indies.

Our first stop was here on the Island of Antigua, I had studied a book entitled, "See the Caribbean for $5 Per Day." Listed in the book was a hotel at St. Johns, Antigua, Anxious to save God's money entrusted to us, we made reservations bit this $5 per day hotel. We arrived in the middle of the night and were driven by taxi to this rickety old hotel. After we registered, we were led upstairs by the light of a candle. It was like something you would read about in a mystery book.

The rooms of the hotel were only separated by partitions that didn't reach the ceiling. In spite of very inferior accommodations, we were exhilarated by the awareness that we were undertaking a new phase of God's calling...in a strange new environment. Having gotten to bed about 2:00 A.M., we were hardly prepared for the sudden invasion of sounds coming from the streets about 5,:00 A.M. The people of the West Indies are famous early risers. As daylight was breaking, the streets below us were filled with the sounds of people and animals on the move. Still, all went well that first day as we got acquainted with the island people and learned they were avid listeners to our daily broadcast.

That night, however, things came unglued. Sleeping under a mosquito net in this dingy little hotel, I developed a high fever. (Later it was diagnosed that my condition was the result of a violent reaction to the smallpox vaccination I had back in Canada.) I became delirious, alternately experiencing cold chills, then raging fevers. The next morning I was weak and exhausted. But we were compelled to persist on with our crusade plans.

When we made our way to another island, en route for our first crusade, I began to experience uncontrollable hemorrhaging from my nose. The manager of the hotel where we were staying thought I was dying. She became terrified at the prospect and asked my wife to get me out of the hotel, for she did not want a dead man on her hands.

A missionary from New York had invited us for our first crusade at an island called Tortola. A phone call to him revealed that he had suddenly departed for New York and was not on the island. This compounded our problems, for our next crusade was not scheduled to begin for some days, and here I was with a badly swollen arm, continuous fevers and hemorrhaging plaguing me.

Finally, in desperation, we decided to give up, cancel our crusade plans and return home. As far as our overseas ministry, we had accomplished absolutely nothing. Zero.

We returned home where my wide and I suffered bleeding bowels for several weeks. However, the awareness that God had called us for overseas crusade ministry did not diminish. We were challenged by the fact that we must return to the West Indies…and to Antigua where I had suffered so much.

The next year an invitation came from the 29 churches of the United Evangelical Association for me to come to Antigua for a crusade. Monster-like fears began to assail me. What if I returned to Antigua and failed again? Would I be beset with physical problems like I had previously encountered? How the fear of failure stalked my path in those days of planning to return to the West Indies.

I had to employ every spiritual weapon I had ever learned to overcome this devastating fear of failure.

Perhaps more than anything else, it was a massive victory over fear that we had even accepted the invitation to go back to Antigua after meeting such dismal defeat the previous year.

But return we did, a victor over the fear of failure, the fear of ill health, the fear of some calamity besetting us.

That crusade was an immense success to the glory and praise of our Lord, with crowds estimated from 8,000 to 17,000 people. This crusade set the stage for future crusades on 22 other islands of the West Indies.

Now, here we are on Antigua, fifteen years after that first journey, achieving daily triumphs of faith.

Here's how we obtained triumph over the fears that beset us:

1. Acting on the hundreds of Bible verses that assured us of freedom from tormenting fears, we began to affirm, "Fear has no part in my heart." What you say is what you get. We said that fear had no part in us; this became wondrous reality.

2. This doesn't mean that we never again were met by opposing forces. Satan had schemed that if he could discourage us after that first setback, that possibly we would never again invade his domain overseas. But Jesus has equipped us by His Word for such combat in the Spirit. Consequently, by His grace we prevailed mightily. We returned to Antigua again and again for crusades. Oppressive forces sought to hinder us, even jeopardizing our safety by threats against us. We employed the same spiritual weapons and conquered in the name of the Lord.

3. The intimidating fear of failure that tried to frustrate us after our first lack of accomplishment was a force to be reckoned with. We maintained our confession of His Word and through the authority of His name we were winners...again and again. This is our thirty-third journey to these islands for ministry! Praise His name!

SATAN TRIES THE SAME TRICKS

Even after the triumph at Antigua, I found myself battling a similar fear of failure when we were invited to make our first trip to India just two years ago.

When the invitation to go to India came from Fran Nelson of Rahway, New Jersey, Joyce and I were not too enthusiastic. We had heard so much about the deplorable conditions in poverty-stricken India that it had little natural appeal. But even more than that, I found myself thinking about the millions of people, their great needs that seemed so far beyond me and their strong roots in Far Eastern religions. How would I fare in such a land?

I remembered the time we had that large crusade in Montreal. The uncontrollable crowds that made it impossible to minister until we evoked the mighty name of Jesus. I began to imagine that the enormous crowds in India could so easily get out of my control. Fears of the unknown assailed me. Would this mission be a failure?

Then the Word of God, my weapon over every fear, took the upper hand. The Lord reminded me that Satan prowls around like a roaring lion, seeking whom he may devour. (See 1 Peter 5:8.) He could try to sneak these fears up on me justifying that I was going to a strange new place, but they were still a product of his evil spirit.

The God reminded me of the overwhelming needs of the Indian people, needs that could only be met by the name and power of Jesus. I was able to look beyond my own fear to the help I could give those people in the wonderful name of Jesus. Acts 4:29, 30, 33 took on a new meaning for me: "Lord, grant unto thy servant, Don Gossett, that with all boldness I may speak thy Word, by stretching forth thine hand to heal, and that signs and wonders might be done in the name of Jesus. And with great power, we may give witness of the resurrection of Jesus, and that great grace will be upon us all."

On November 25, 1979, Joyce and I left Seattle, Washington, on a United flight non-stop to New York City. We flew to London on Air India and then on to India itself. Our first stop was at the national capitol, New Delhi. Then on to Bombay where we had our first look at what we had heard about so often…dear people, especially little children, sleeping on the streets, beggars lined up in our pathway. We went to the hotel where we took a much-desired shower, changed clothes and departed for Nagercoil and the sight of our first crusade.

We were not prepared for the natural beauty of India. The rain forests, the rice paddies, the water and mountains…all blended together to assure us that God didn't bypass India when he created scenery that was breath-taking.

But the most impressive sight about India was the people. People everywhere; from the time we landed at Bombay, in all the villages, alongside the country roads-people, people, people everywhere.

These were people for whom Jesus died, and this was the object of our coming…to win as many of these precious people to the Son of God that we possibly could.

Less than 24 hours later, our crusade in Nagercoil began.

After the introduction of team members, I was invited to come and share my first gospel message to the waiting multitudes, my first preaching assignment in India! Clearly I told of the benefits of knowing Jesus Christ as Savior and Lord. My text was Psalm 103:1-5. After 40 minutes of speaking through my excellent Tamul interpreter. Brother David, I gave my first invitation for the people of India to accept our Savior! Eagerly the people stood over the park. I was aware that the prayers of God's people everywhere were being answered, as the Holy Spirit was touching hearts and people were ready to receive our Lord by faith!

I led the people in the "sinners' prayer" of repentance and acceptance of Jesus. I then asked that whoever knew for certain they were saved to indicate it by raising both hands in surrender to the Lordship of Jesus. Without hesitation they did so. Then personal workers moved quickly with convert cards to hand to those who had just accepted the Lord. They were also offered Tamul New Testaments and given an invitation to come to the New Converts meeting the following morning.

This was to be the pattern of ministry night after night in each service. The Lord permitted me to preach a strong, anointed message on salvation. A report was given at the end of the crusades that more than 100,000 persons received Jesus Christ as Savior and Lord. Only God knows for certain how many were truly born again by faith in Jesus. God is the great Record Keeper who knows His own.

MIRACLE SERVICE

So great were the crowds that it was impossible to personally lay hands on the sick for healing. I carefully explained from God's Word why they could receive a healing miracle as I prayed in the name of Jesus.

I had fortified myself with the grand passages of John 14:13-14. There Jesus promised, "*Whatsoever ye shall ask in my name, that will I do, that the Father may be glorified in the Son. If ye shall ask anything in my name, I will do it.*" Many years ago, I had learned that the word *"ask"* in this passage actually means to "demand or command."

In that very first miracle service, people came to the platform to share their testimonies of tremendous miracles. Two different persons who had been carried to the crusade with crippled limbs demonstrated decisively how the Lord had ministered healing. They could walk, run and use their limbs with total freedom! The second night I focused on the deaf. For several minutes I invoked the name of Jesus in commanding deafness to come out of ears and hearing to come in! Praise God, people came forward whose deaf ears had been opened! How the people rejoiced at these miracles plus many others.

I encountered almost every kind of disease known to mankind in India. The needs of the people were so vast. When I traveled for five years with evangelist William Freeman in his large salvation healing campaigns; in America, I saw long lines of sick people. But the poor, disadvantaged people of India are so much worse than any crowd of suffering people in more privileged America.

To witness the abnormalities of their bodies was a heartbreaking experience. Yet the power and authority of the Lord's majestic name was equal to all their sufferings. My confidence had to be only in His name. Boldly, and with compassion, I would speak out His great name to combat and heal the sickness of the people.

After several more days of ministering to India's dear people, the hour came when we met at the airport for our departure. We bade the beloved brethren goodbye

As our plane was airborne, I looked down on the lovely rice paddies, the towering mountains, and the rivers where people were washing clothes and bathing. But the sight I could see most distinctly was people...the precious people to whom God had sent us.

I understood why Satan had tried so deliberately to stop us through fears of failure. God had a tremendous work of mercy and saving grace to do in India. Praise His name for the great works He has wrought in India and the glorious victory over our personal fears. I can joyfully join in with the psalmist, *"Behold, God is my salvation; I will trust, and not be afraid: for the LORD JEHOVAH is my strength and my song; he also is become my salvation. Therefore with joy shall ye draw water out of the wells of salvation. And in that day shall ye say, Praise the LORD, call upon his name, declare his doings among the people, make mention that his name is exalted. Sing unto the LORD; for he hath done excellent things: this is known in all the earth"* (Isaiah 12:2-5).

11

THE RISING COST OF FEAR

Many people today are being harassed in their financial situations. They fear the possibilities of spiraling inflation, a major recession or both!

So often, Satan takes advantage of the financial anxieties of life and brings his choice spirits of fear to torment, to snare, to bring all kinds of difficulties. Indeed, the matter of finances is Re any other situation. What you fear is what you get! If you give place to the fear of financial failure you can invite that failure to come and grip your life.

I want to share with you the true, story of a businessman who overcame the dreaded spirit of fear, but not before it nearly cost him everything he had. This man had been in business for many years, and he had known real success. But then he began to be oppressed by a fear of failure; a fear of financial disruption. In fact, a fear of bankruptcy itself. I want to share his testimony with you as he has written it himself:

> I had been a retail clothier in a community of 5,000 people for more than 35 years when adversity laid its blighting hand upon me.
>
> My son and daughter were in a large university depending upon me to meet their expenses when a

bank failure tied up all my funds and cut off my bor-
rowing privileges. I was right up against the buzz saw.
Then the next day the sheriff came in with a delinquent
tax bill, which I could not pay. The only thing left was
bankruptcy.

My wife and I were much in prayer, pinning our faith
on such passages as Isaiah 41:10: *"Fear thou not; for I
am with thee: be not dismayed; for I am thy God: I will
strengthen thee; yea, I will help thee; yea, I will uphold thee
with the right hand of my righteousness."* Then the hour
came to test our faith.

It was a hot, sultry day in August. As I left home that
morning, my wife kissed me goodbye, and, holding fast
to my coat lapel, said, "Now, Honey, don't worry. God
will take care of us, some way." But I could see no pos-
sible way out.

At ten o'clock that morning, in the lawyer's office, I
signed a writ of voluntary bankruptcy. Then I went back
to the store where the Creditor's Committee had been
busy all morning invoicing the stock. At twelve o'clock
they and the clerks left for lunch.

Alone in the store, I stood behind the neckwear
showcase, about midway from the front, reflecting on
my many years of striving. I thought of the prosperous
years, of the ups and downs of business life. And: now I
was about to say farewell to all my plans and dreams and
push out into a cold world without a job and without
money!

I thought of my beloved wife who had stood by me through the years, of my son and daughter whose college life would have to be terminate, at least for the present.

As I stood there, I was convinced of my sin of fearing financial defeat. I began praising God, thanking Him for our good health and the privilege of depending on Him for anew start.

And then—at twelve fifteen—*God walked in the door.*

I say this reverently because to me it could have been none other than God in the person of my keenest competitor. He rarely came into our store. We were not on the same social or religious plane-just casual friends.

He walked up to me and said, "What's this I hear about you declaring bankruptcy?" I told him it was a solemn fact. He looked at me questioningly and asked, "Is there no way out?"

"I don't see any," I replied.

"We simply cannot let this happen." He said. "You are one of our best town boosters." He quietly reached into his pocket and handed me a sizable check, saying, "Would this change the picture?"

Stunned, and with tears in my eyes, I said, "Yes, I'm quite sure it will."

Of all the friends I had in the city, this man was the very last I ever expected would do a thing like that. The others were sorry—just sorry—but he was sorry with "money that talks."

Who put it into this man's heart to come to my aid at that crucial hour? Nobody but God, who all the time had been standing within the shadow keeping watch over His own. He waited for my decision to put aside my fears and place my trust in Him. Then He answered my faith in a dramatic way.

The years that followed were successful and prosperous. With God's further help, I was able to pay my competitor back in full, with interest, in a short time.

—*Charles Clifford Wescott*

One, sure way of conquering the fear of financial defeat is God's Word on giving from Malachi 3:8-11:

"Will a man rob God? Yet ye have robbed me. But ye say, wherein have we robbed thee? In tithes and offerings.... Bring ye all the tithes into the storehouse, that there may be meat in mine house, and prove me now herewith, saith the LORD of hosts, if I will not open you the windows of heaven, and pour you out a blessing, that there shall not be room enough to receive it. And I will rebuke the devourer for your sakes, and he shall not destroy the fruits of your ground; neither shall your vine cast her fruit before the time in the field, saith the LORD of hosts."

By standing on the Word of God and obeying it in giving our tithes and offerings, we can defeat the devourer's attacks on our finances. We can meet and defeat Satan by saying, "My God has promised to open the gates of heaven and pour out a greater blessing than I can receive. Satan, be gone, in Jesus's name!"

This is how one man learned that even fearful circumstances *cannot break God's promise* made to those who tithe.

Alexander H. Kerr was converted under the ministry of Dwight L. Moody at the age of 14 and joined the Presbyterian Church at Philadelphia. In 1902, Mr. Kerr read a book entitled *Judah's Scepter and Joseph's Birthright,* by Bishop Allen.

In his book, Bishop Allen referred to the vow Jacob made in Genesis 28:22 where we find the following words: *"Of all that thou shalt give me, I will surely give the tenth unto thee."*

Twenty years later this same Jacob returned to his home with servants and cattle in great abundance; thus, her became one of the richest men of the east as a result of keeping his covenant of tithing with the Lord God.

With some doubts, but with a sincere desire to see if the Bible is true, to prove without a shadow of doubt that there is a personal God and, that His promises are intended for people of this day Mr. Kerr, on June 1, 1902, made a special covenant to set aside the tithe, or 10 percent of his income for the work of the Lord.

At that time he had a mortgage on his little home, owed many obligations, and was burdened with cares and worries, especially of a financial nature. However, he was determined to prove God as did Jacob. He was also challenged by these Scriptures: Proverbs 3:9-10; Leviticus 27:30-32; Genesis 14:20, 1 13:2; and especially Malachi 3:7-18.

Mr. Kerr often remarked that if modem day skeptics wanted proof that there is a God, and that the Bible is His Holy Word and all its promises are true, all that is necessary is to tithe for one year, and God will prove to them without a doubt that He is *"the same yesterday, and today, and forever"* (Hebrews 13:8).

Within three months after Mr. Kerr began to tithe, unexpected and unforeseen blessings came to him so much so that it seemed that God had opened his eyes to behold His love and His faithfulness to His promises, especially made in regard to tithing.

"ACCORDING TO YOUR FAITH BE IT UNTO YOU" (MATTHEW 9:29)

That same year Mr. Kerr, with very little capital but with strong faith in God's tithing promises contained in Malachi 3:10-12 organized the firm known as the Kerr Glass Manufacturing Company which became one of the largest firms selling fruit jars in the United States.

The jars were manufactured for him in San Francisco. At the time of the San Francisco earthquake, this firm was manufacturing his fruit jars.

Mr. Kerr had put practically every cent he had in the world into this fruit jar enterprise, and then came the earthquake! His friends came to him and said: "Kerr, you are a ruined man." He replied, I don't believe it; or if I am, then the Bible is not true; I know God will not go back on His promises." He wired to San Francisco, and received the following reply:

"Your factory is in the heart of the fire and undoubtedly is destroyed. The heat is so intense we will be unable to find out anything for, some days."

"I will rebuke the devourer for your sakes, and he shall not destroy the fruits of your ground" (Malachi 3:11).

What a time of testing this was! But Mr. Kerr's faith in the Lord never wavered. He believed Malachi 3:11 and stood on this promise, unmoved. About a week after the earthquake and fire, a second telegram, arrived saying:

"Everything for a mile and a half on all sides of the factory burned; but your factory miraculously saved."

GOD'S WORD CANNOT RETURN UNTO HIM VOID (ISAIAH 55:8-11)

Mr. Kerr immediately boarded a train for San Francisco. The factory was a two-story wooden building containing the huge tanks where the glass was melted. The tanks were kept at a fierce 2,500 degrees and oil was used for fuel. Therefore, this building was probably the most flammable in San Francisco.

The fire had raged on all sides of this glass factory, creeping up to the wooden fence surrounding the building and even scorching it; then the flames and fire leaped around and over and beyond the building, burning everything in its path. However, not even the wooden fence was burned, nor the building, and not a single glass jar was cracked by earthquake or fire!

This was nothing short of a miracle of God's divine power in protecting this man who held his faith that God's promises made to those who tithe would never be broken by any circumstances!

In 1912, Mr. Kerr wrote his first leaflet on the subject of tithing, entitled "God's Cure for Poverty." This was followed by another tract entitled, "God's Loving Money Rule for Your Financial Prosperity." Every case of fruit jars that left the factory contained one of these leaflets.

He advertised to give them away to people who would judiciously scatter them-bearing the entire cost himself. From 1912 to the time of his death, February 9, 1924, he had freely distributed more than five million of these leaflets!

Three weeks before his death he addressed the members of the First Baptist Church of Riverside, California, on the blessings and riches of tithing possessions, income and increase. Every business in which he had an investment tithed.

His returns were so great that he created a Tithing fund and has it incorporated. His tithing gifts went around the world, for he was deeply interested in the distribution of testaments, gospels, and gospel literature.

He rose from poverty to millions because he *believed* that God would honor His promise to pour our His blessings today upon those who would accurately and carefully tithe or set aside one-tenth of their possessions, salary or income for the Lord's work.

Do you have a fear financially? Are you afraid to give? I challenge you. Let the Lord give you a release from the fear of financial failure that can often stare you in the face and cause you loss of sleep. Let's pray about it shall we?

"Father, I ask in the name of Jesus for the release from financial distress for every friend united with me right now. Father, you know how real this fear is, the fear of financial disaster, and the fear of inability to pay bills, the fear of bankruptcy. I ask you to bring deliverance to every captive life. And I pray that the spirit of fear will be expelled. For you have said, "Fear not, for I am with thee.' Thank you, Lord, for your release, in Jesus's mighty name. Amen." Now receive your release and move on to Prosperity!

12

A CONFIDENT CONFESSION

A dearly loved man of God, Dr. E. W. Kenyon, once related this little story; "Years ago, I knew a man who started out in business with every promise of success. He had the right location. He had the right kind of business. He had a multitude of friends. He was a good buyer and a good salesman.

"I went into his store on my way to the post office, nearly every morning. I used to admire his store. It was so clean. The details were so carefully managed.

"Slowly, a change came over him. He had a little domestic difficulty. He began to talk fearfully, discouragingly. In two years that man talked himself out of a splendid, growing business.

"I did not know then what I know now, or I could have stopped him. He simply talked himself out. He discouraged people who came in. He was full of pessimism and fear. He challenged everything. Finally, he talked himself into absolute failure."

You cannot afford to talk failure, doubt or fear. Why? Because words register in your heart and after they have registered, they take control of your life.

"Thou hast confessed a good confession, before many witnesses" (1 Timothy 6:12).

A good confession or a bad confession, which will it be? You are ruled by your confession. You are today exactly a product of what you've been believing and confessing.

A good confession is the forerunner of good outcomes and results. A bad confession, based on fear, is the forerunner of bad outcomes.

Fear confession: "Well, I made it to work today, but that's about all I can say. The way I feel, I certainly don't expect to get much done."

Confident confession: "No, no, no! I refuse to give place to a gloomy confession. That would thoroughly snare my soul. *'Thou art snared with the words of thy mouth'* (Proverbs 6:2).

"I serve God continually, so I am assured of deliverance from that pessimistic attitude of fear that would crush my spirit and defeat my soul. *'Thy God whom thou servest continually, he will deliver thee'* (Daniel 6:16). God is my deliverer in every case, for I serve Him constantly.

"On my job, in my service for the Lord, whatever I do…I am more than a conqueror through Christ who loves me. (See Romans 8:37.) I reject that barely-able-to-keep-my-head-above-water attitude.

"The Lord is showing me great and mighty things about my life. Why? Because He has said to me, *'Call unto me, and I will answer thee, and show thee great and mighty things, which thou knowest not'* (Jeremiah 33:3). I call unto Him, He is answering me, and showing me great and mighty things! I refuse to be bound by poor attitudes that would cause me to confess despairingly."

It's highly important that we have a good mental attitude as welt as a strong confession if we are to be achievers in life. The people who are failures are characterized by poor attitudes and soul-snaring words. The Lord want s us to come forth with bright, optimistic outlooks and confessions. Thus, we shall prevail.

Fear confession: "I failed to get that promotion I hoped for. But it's just as I expected, as I never seem to succeed at anything."

Confident confession: "I don't believe that adverse forces are overthrowing God's working in my behalf. The Lord is even working on, the answers before I pray. *'Before they call, I will answer; and while they are yet speaking, I will hear'* (Isaiah 65:24). I do not fear bad outcomes. I fully expect success instead of failure. Jesus didn't come to give me a puny, failing life. *'I am come that they might have life, and that they might have it more abundantly'* (John 10:10). Because I have received Jesus Christ as my personal Savior and Lord, I have that abundant life in me now.

"I just know God is prospering my life. *'Beloved, I wish above all things that thou mayest prosper and be in health, even as thy soul prospereth'* (3 John 2). I have a right to prosperity and health, because I am prospering in my soul.

"God has promised to bless me richly, even materially, right in this life, because I am a giver. Jesus said, *'Give, and it shall be given unto you; good measure, pressed down, and shaken together, and running over, shall men give into your bosom'* (Luke 6:38). Ah yes, the Lord is heaping up my blessings for I am giving unto Him and His work. No negative hopeless testimony for me: I am blessed!"

God's Word so thoroughly promises us success in every area of life that it's a pity that anyone should confess failure and defeat. To confess an injurious confession is like taking a dose of poison in your inner man. It is sheer defeatism that will reap in kind. As we continue to sow words of confidence in God's Word, we reap a harvest of blessings.

Fear confession: "I don't dare attempt this particular task as it is beyond my ability."

Confident confession: "My ability is measured by God's ability. *'If God be for us, who can be against us'* (Romans 8:31). God is really for me; so I can do all things through Him Who is my strength and sufficiency. (See Philippians 4:13.) I never minimize my ability, for I know the truth and the truth sets me free. (See John 8:32.) I am absolutely made strong with His strength. *'Let the weak say, I am strong'* (Joel 3:10). I say it boldly, "I am strong right in the face of supposed weakness.'

"I count on the mighty One who quickens my mortal body. *'He that raised up Christ from the dead shall also quicken your mortal bodies by his Spirit that dwelleth in you'* (Romans 8:1 1). God quickens my mortal body now by the very same Spirit that raised Jesus from the dead, because His Spirit dwells in me. Thus, I can face any task and succeed because His Spirit dwells in me. Thus, I can face any task and succeed because of His unlimited ability within me. Hallelujah!"

As Christians we learn to rely upon the supernatural ability of God. Natural ability is important. But there is no substitute fir relying upon divine life, divine anointing, and divine strength for every situation.

Fear confession: "I probably will not be able to go. I'm sure that I won't have the money in time."

Confident confession: "I never defeat myself by fearfully forecasting failure in advance for my life. I refuse to entertain pessimism about any of my life's plans. Jesus has given me some great assurances about life. He declares, *'Everyone that asketh receiveth'* (Matthew 7:8). Everyone includes me. I know I am receiving those good and needful things from the Lord, because I have asked Him. Thus, I am receiving, for His promise contains no exceptions.

"I am carefree about the future, for I have joyfully cast all of my cares upon Him who really cares for me. (See 1 Peter 5:7.) I am sure that God supplies all the money I need…and in plenty of time to minister to my needs. I praise His name!"

How sad are the multitudes of people, even Christians, who face life with a defeatist attitude. Their expectation is one of continual lack, restriction, and deficiency. What a contrast is the attitude to face life with the optimistic assurance of good outcomes.

⌒

Fear confession: "I don't know what I will do if the cost of living keeps going up."

Confident confession: "I live by the Word of God, *'My God shall supply all my need according to His riches in glory by Christ Jesus'* (Philippians, 4:19). Regardless of inflation my need, God shall minister to all my need.

"Psalm 1 promises, *'Blessed is the man that walketh not in the counsel of the ungodly, nor standeth in the way of sinners, nor sitteth in the seat of the scornful. But his delight is in the law of the LORD, and in his law doth he meditate day and night. And he shall be like a tree planted by the rivers of water, that bringeth forth his fruit in his season; his leaf also shall not wither; and whatsoever he doeth shall prosper.'*

"I personalize this promise to my life and affirm these words.

"I walk not in the counsel of the ungodly. I stand not in the way of sinners. I sit not in the seat of the scornful. I delight myself in the word of God. Both day and night I meditate on it. I am like a tree planted by the waters. I am bearing fruit. As a result, whatsoever I do shall prosper!

"If the cost of living keeps going up, God's prospering of my life shall increase. I do not fear inflation; the Lord is my supply!"

As Christians we have a choice to either live by the Word or by the ruling circumstances of the day. If we focus our attention upon the problems of inflation, those problems will sap vitality out of our spirits. But if we focus our attention on God's never failing Word, he shall be our supply in the face of fluctuating living costs.

Fear confession: "Why does this always have to happen to me?"

Confident confession: "I expect nothing evil or bad to happen to me. I live by the words of the promise. *'There shall no evil befall thee, neither shall any plague come nigh thy dwelling'* (Psalm 91:10).

"God commands me to *'Commit thy way unto the LORD; trust also in him; and he shall bring it to pass'* (Psalm 37:5). I expect Him to bring to pass good outcomes, not bad ones. I refuse to moan about the possibility of bad things happening to me because He has promised, *'The, Lord shall deliver me from every evil work'* (2 Timothy 4:18). As a sincere Christian, I seek to walk uprightly before Him. He assures me, 'No good thing will he withhold from them that walk uprightly' (Psalm 84:11). Something good always happens to me!"

How about you? God has given you all things that pertain to life and godliness. (See 2 Peter 1:3.) He has blessed you with all spiritual blessings in the heavenly places in Christ. (See Ephesians 1:3.) God is the giver of every good and every perfect gift. (See James 1:17.) God delights to give richly all things for your enjoyment. (See 1 Timothy 6:17.) The Bible declares all things are yours, and you are Christ's. (See 1 Corinthians 3:21,23.)

Are you praising God for these wonderful gifts, which are yours? Or are you making a fearful confession? Cease glorifying your defeats your lack, your sickness, and begin to glorify God in your victories your supply, your health. It is high time to convert your fearful excuses into testimonies!

Boldly affirm the Scriptures that assure of conquest in all spiritual battles, and you will experience them. Be hesitant and fearful about your provisions in Christ and you will be defeated.

The bolder your confession of faith, the greater will be your victories.

Praise God for all things that are yours. Not "I wish I was blessed," but saying, "I am blessed with all spiritual blessings in Christ Jesus!" Hallelujah, it is so!

Confess your riches in Christ, then posses your possessions!

WHAT I CONFESS I POSSESS

1. I confess Jesus as my Lord (see Romans 10:9-10); I possess salvation.

2. I confess, "by His stripes I am healed" (see Isaiah 53:5); I possess healing.

3. I confess "the Son has made me free" (see John 8:36). I possess absolute freedom.

4. I confess "the love of God is shed abroad in my heart by the Holy Ghost" (see Romans 5:5); I possess the ability to love everyone.

5. I confess, "the righteous are bold as a lion" (see Proverbs 28:1); I possess lion-hearted boldness in spiritual warfare.

6. I confess, "he will never leave me nor forsake me" (see Hebrews 13:5); I possess the presence of God each step I take.

7. I confess, "I am the redeemed of the Lord" (see Psalm 107:2); I possess redemption every day.

8. I confess, "the anointing of the Holy One abideth in me" (see 1 John 2:27); I possess yoke-destroying results by this anointing (see Isaiah 10:27).

9. I confess "in the name of Jesus I can cast out devils " (see Mark 16:17); I possess dynamic deliverances as a devil-master.

10. I confess, "I lay my hands on the sick, and they shall recover" (see Mark 16:18); I possess positive healings for the oppressed.

11. I confess, "I am a branch of the living Vine" (see John 15:5); I possess Vine-Life wherever I go.

12. I confess, "I am the righteousness of God in Christ" (see 2 Corinthians 5:21); I possess the ability to stand

freely in God's holy presence and in Satan's presence as a victor!

13. I confess, "I am a temple of the living God" (see 2 Corinthians 6:16); I possess God dwelling in me, and walking in me!

14. I confess "my God shall supply all my need" (see Philippians 4:19); I possess the supply for every need!

15. I confess, "God has not given me a spirit of fear; but of power, and love, and of a sound mind" (see 2 Timothy 1:7); I possess the courage and strength to live a life free from all fears!

13

A GREATER POWER
THAN FEAR

Ray Anderson had been a Christian for only two months when he and his wife, Ellen, started to Bible school for two years of training. After becoming grounded in the Word and knowing that the call of God upon their lives was real, the Andersons were strongly impressed to go to Kenya, East Africa, as missionaries.

Knowing that their needs would be as real as their calling, and realizing that they would be encountering every kind of disease known to man, as well as meeting with demon power, they went forth in the Lord.

For about a year they worked in Kenya. Their small daughter, Christi, stayed with them on the mission compound. Ray and Ellen had no doubt that God had called them to Africa to do a work for Him. Yet, even though they knew being obedient to the call of God might mean going through the valley of the shadow of death, they did not anticipate how real that valley of death could be.

Many things, kept reminding them that they were in Africa, The slow movements of the people. The throngs of blacks.

The open market places, where flies infested both meats and vegetables. A totally different culture. Then there were the evening sounds, strange to their ears…drums, chanting, the roar of the lion, the trumpet of an elephant. The smells one could never mistake nor forget. Also, they were constantly aware of the country because of the totally different way of eating; the main diet was milled corn, rice, half-cooked chicken and river water tea. It wasn't exactly the same as the savory food from the States!

Soon, the Anderson's became accustomed to working in this foreign land. They began to concentrate on training national pastors. These pastors were natives of East Africa who had been called to minister to their own people.

Two lingering marks will forever remind Ray Anderson of those days in Kenya. One is a hole in the left side of his Land Rover and the other is a scar on his left side.

The day began as any other day with its variety of sights and smells. Then, a messenger came to report that one of the national pastors had sold a bicycle that had been assigned to him in carrying the gospel of Jesus Christ. For the man to have sold what was not his made him, a thief, and stealing was considered a very serious offense. Just a small act like this could result in a lengthy prison term. Ray Anderson, as head missionary, had his work cut out for him to find the pastor and to discover who had the bicycle,

Ray and his interpreter drove the Land Rover deep into the bush of Kenya. The missionary hoped fervently that he not only could find out who now possessed the bicycle, but help the brother who had gold it. It took several hours of snaking through the bush before they pulled in front of the pastor's hut. It appeared that he had been sitting there, just waiting for them to come. Because Ray knew the procedure he must follow, he had brought two policemen from the village along with him.

Ray counseled with the national pastor for some minutes, hoping he would simply disclose the location of the bicycle and all could be cleared up quickly. But the pastor would not supply the men with any information, and the police began to grow impatient.

"It will be much easier for you if you will just tell us, where the bicycle is," Ray pled through his interpreter. "We want to help you, not hurt you. As a brother in Christ, we—"

The policemen moved restlessly. "Put him in the Rover. We're taking him to the chief," they ordered.

Whether the words struck fear in his heart, or whether an evil spirit attacked him, no one could ever be quite sure why the national pastor began to react as he did.

In an instant the man displayed great violence. He smashed his fist into the mouth of one of the policemen and screamed, "There's going to be, blood shed here today."

Breaking free, the man ran into his hut and locked the door. The police tried in vain to get inside. Seconds later he burst out of the hut carrying a spear in his right hand. The spear was poised and held high in the air. He was a tall man and an expert spear thrower. "I'm going to kill you! I'm going to kill you!"

"Run!" shouted Ray's interpreter. "He is really going to kill you!"

When Ray looked around he discovered that the national pastor had run into the bush. Not knowing where the man was, Ray knew he was an open target. Fear began rising inside of him, fear as he had never known in his life. It was a breathless consuming force, without reason or limit. Blindly, Ray dashed to the Land Rover and around it. Seconds later, the national was right behind him, long legs filling the space between them, spear poised high for a throw. Those powerful muscles behind the spear could send it straight through Ray's body.

Ray fell, got up and ran again. He fell again, his feet slipping on the wet grass. It was insanity, a nightmare filled with torment and stark reality. The door of the Land Rover was partly open and Ray made a grab for it. His heart was pounding like the drums at night. It hammered through his head and raced in crazy waves through his entire nervous system. His lungs screamed for air.

He turned his head in time to see the spear leave the man's hand in a mighty surge of power. In that split second, while the spear raced through the air, thoughts tumbled rapidly through Ray's whirling brain. Without thinking or planning, his hand grabbed the door of the Land Rover as he stumbled. The door swung wide, blocking die initial force of the spear. Ray was almost on his feet and beginning to run again when the spear came through the door and struck him in the side. It was a superficial wound and Ray drove his body into another dead run. The bleeding wasn't too great, but Ray knew he had been wounded.

The national pulled the spear from its position and in an instant was right behind the missionary.

The fear Ray was experiencing was of such an overwhelming magnitude that he began Sobbing and calling out to God. It was unexplainable, what was happening to him. He had cast out devils and encountered many situations where great courage was necessary, even imperative. But this fear was a force he had never encountered before.

"Help me, Jesus! God, help me!"

As total exhaustion gripped his body, a miracle began taking place. The cavities of fear were being filled with faith. He stopped running. It was as though he could feel himself growing taller, and stronger. Facing his enemy, his hand went up and he cried, "Jesus! Jesus! Jesus! Jesus!"

Ray was trembling from the power that had come upon him. He faced his opponent without a trace of fear. The national stopped. He began to shake and tremble, and the spear fell from his hand as a child might drop a toy. The terrible ordeal was over.

Ray Anderson saw this national pastor just once, after that, when he came and asked forgiveness, and together they wept and prayed; then the man disappeared from the authorities and has not been seen since. If he were caught, it would mean approximately twenty-one years in prison for all that he had done.

For Ray, this near tragedy has built his faith higher than ever before, for he now knows the reality of what Paul wrote to Timothy: "God hath not given us the spirit of fear; but of power, and of love, and of a sound mind."

Seven years have passed since this experience. Ray has returned from the bush country of East Africa, where he witnessed much fruit for his labor. Over one hundred and fifty churches have been established in the bush country. To date, the man who speared Ray has not returned to his home. Before Ray and Ellen left Kenya, they took food and clothing to his family. The message of their giving and concern for others echoed through the bush. Today there now stands a church with a strong congregation. Truly there is greater Power!

Many of the youth who accepted Jesus Christ into their lives then are now Pastors in remote areas of the bush.

While it is true, there are two lingering marks which will remind Ray Anderson of those days in Kenya," there remains yet another mark which, will also remind him. It is not a visible mark seen with human eyes, but rather a mark engraved within his heart,

A mark that penetrates one's very soul. A mark that tells him, there is a greater power!

FEAR HATH TORMENT

There are several important factors about the testimony of Ray Anderson, which apply to any person held captive by fear.

1. Ray Anderson was literally in the snare of the fear of man. *"The fear of man bringeth a snare: but whoso putteth his trust in the LORD shall be safe"* (Proverbs 29:25). When Ray was opposed by his towering national, he was suddenly gripped by an intense fear of this man. His soul was snared, trapped. Ray stated, "Fear began rising inside of me, fear as I had never known in my entire life. It was a breathless, consuming force, without reason or limit." I ask you: Are you snared by the fear of man? You would speak up for Jesus Christ, but you are afraid of the opposition of people. You'd be used of God in ministering healing to a sick person, but the fear of others' opinions forbids you from bold ministry in Jesus's name.

2. Another type of fear Ray Anderson experienced was the fear of an untimely death. As he was fleeing for his life, he said, "It was insanity, a nightmare filled with torment and stark reality." 1 John 4:18 says, *"Fear hath torment."* Many of God's children today are experiencing the torment of fear. The fear of cancer, of a heart attack, or some deadly disease.

Through the authority of Jesus's name, there is freedom from fears that torment. Dare to speak His name for your release.

The total release for Ray came when he followed the pattern of the man, David, in the Bible. David testified, *"I sought the Lord, and he heard me, and delivered me from all my fears"* (Psalm 34:4). It was not weakness to call out to God as Ray did when it appeared there was no hope for his life. "The fear that he was experiencing was of such overwhelming magnitude that he began sobbing and calling out to God…. This fear was a force he had never encountered before."

Ray cried, "Help me, Jesus! God, help me!"

You can't beat that method of overcoming fear, simply calling unto the Lord: *"The name of the Lord is a strong tower, the righteous runneth into it, and is safe"* (Proverbs 18:10).

The climax of Ray's deliverance came when he faced his enemy and cried, "Jesus! Jesus! Jesus! Jesus!" Oh, there's something about that name! Something that causes demons to fear, causes fears to vanish!

14

PROTECTION BY DAY AND NIGHT

The very spirit of this age is one of tension, and with the crisis in world affairs constantly intensifying, we are reminded that Jesus spoke, *"Men's hearts are failing them for fear, and for looking after those things which are coming on the earth"* (Luke 21:26).

I have found that one thing people greatly fear is physical harm, whether it is from catastrophic events, other people or even some animals. But Christians can rest in God's Word in the face of all sorts of threats against their well-being.

I would like to challenge you now with the following stories from some of our friends in the ministry. Stand strong against fear for God is your protector!

THE FEAR OF RAPE

Mrs. Claire Cudak shares a remarkable testimony of protection against robbery or worse, simply because she was "a child of the King." Here is her own testimony:

"I opened the car door, grabbed my pocketbook and the envelope with the money we had collected for Leonard's going away gift, and was about to get out of my, car when a voice said, 'If you move, I'll put a bullet into your head!'

"I turned my head slightly and saw a gun pointed at my head. Was it real, or was it an air pistol like those my father and brother used in the basement target range at home? The cold steel barrel looked ominously real.

"It was ironic. Many co-workers were not going to bother getting Leonard a gift because he had not endeared himself to them, but I didn't think it was fair. We had done it for everyone who had left in the past. I would make sure that a parting kindness would be his, even if I had to see to it myself.

"Now my Christian concern had gotten me under a gun!

"It suddenly dawned on me that robbery might not be the only thing this young man had in mind. He hadn't asked for my money, and it was very, obvious what was in the envelope with all the names and contributions marked and totaled.

"If it wasn't robbery, was it rape? Oh, God, help me, I prayed. My stomach began to flip flop.

"If he gets in, this car it's robbery, rape, or both; of it could go even beyond that. Would I be murdered, too?

"Then I thought, 'Wait a minute; he's got some nerve! Who does he think he is? I'm a child of the King, and my Heavenly Father takes care of me. How dare he threaten me?'

"Perhaps it was anger, or perhaps God put me on a spiritual automatic pilot. At any rate, it wasn't bravery!

"I deliberately got out of the car. He was forced to back up a little as I got out. 'Do you think I'm kidding?' he menaced. I pushed the lock button down, shut the car door, and walked toward the store.

"I didn't know if I was about to get a bullet in the head or not. But as I walked I said to myself, 'I would just as soon be shot in the parking lot as raped or possibly murdered in some desolate place. Besides, I am a princess, a daughter of the most high God, a child of the King.'

"I walked into the busy store, safe! I reported the incident to the security force at the store. Within a few minutes a policeman was recording all the details. He finally asked if I would mind taking a ride in the patrol, car with him, just in case I might be able to identify the man if we could find him by cruising around the neighborhood.

"I agreed, but honestly hoped I would never see that young man again. We drove for a little while, and then a voice squawked over the radio, 'Man with gun seen in the vicinity of...'

"The car lurched, the siren screamed, the lights flashed on, and off we careened, across oncoming traffic, down a side street. I think I was more frightened now than when menaced with the gun.

"Blocks later, the light and siren were turned off, and we proceeded slowly along the streets. 'I want you to watch carefully and let me know if you see him,' the officer said. I nodded.

"Looking down my side of the street, I didn't see anyone like him. What a relief!

"Then I looked down the other side of the street, and there he was, big as life, "that's him,' I managed to get out.

"The patrol car swung to the curb, the officer leaped out, and drew his gun: 'Freeze!' he shouted. Another patrol car roared up out of nowhere, and two more officers, guns drawn, got out to assist. They took a paper bag from the man. It contained a gun.

"He was taken to the police station. I was asked to come, make a statement and sign a deposition. I don't hate the young man; I pray for his salvation. But it was discovered later, and written in the papers, that he had done this type of thing, and worse, in the past. Perhaps someday he will also become a child of the King.

"For me, looking back, I realize that God did indeed answer my cry for help. Without my realizing what was happening, my reactions changed from fear paralysis to faith actions.

"Perhaps under different circumstances another time, another man, or a different place what I did might have been fatal, but for that incident it was exactly the thing to do. Had I yielded, I might not be writing this. We are children of the King. Every prince and princess gets scared sometimes, but then we can say, with the psalmist, *'What time I am afraid, I will trust in thee'* (Psalm 56:3). He is always with us!"

THE FEAR OF WAR

One woman who fought fear with prayer and the Word of God was Mrs. Mabel Chapman of Burnaby, British Columbia. Mrs. Chapman was born and raised in Great Britain, then moved to Regina, Saskatchewan, Canada, where she and her husband and two sons lived for many years.

When World War II came, Mrs. Chapman's sons entered the Canadian Armed Services. Soon they were shipped off to Europe to be a part of some of the most intense battles of the European theatre. Often, as she would hear news reports of the massive killings of thousands of soldiers, Mrs. Chapman found every reason to be fearful and anxious. Those were her only two sons and she loved them so.

However, with a dear prayer partner in Regina, Mrs. Chapman decided to take a stand against fear and for the safe homecoming of her boys. The two women took bold steps of faith in proclaiming specific Scriptures for her sons that God would protect them and bring them back to her. Included was Psalm 27:3, "Though a host should encamp against me, my heart shall not fear: though war shall rise up against me, in this I will be confident."

As a result of her times of fervent prayer, the Holy Spirit gave Mabel Chapmen a clear promise that her sons would be back home.

Four years went by and she never saw the faces of her sons. When World War II was over, one son came home quickly. She was still confident the other one would be home. When it was announced that the last, troop train was coming to Regina, Mrs. Chapman was there with hundreds of other residents to welcome home the final soldiers. Mrs. Chapman's oldest son had not arrived, and she has often described to me her great anticipation as she continued to confess God's promise that both her sons would be home. When the train pulled into the station, the Regina band struck up a hearty welcome to the soldiers. When they marched into the large train station where the townspeople were waiting, leading the entire procession was Mrs. Chapman's oldest son! God had answered this mother's confident prayers. Both her sons came home!

Mabel Chapman has been a precious friend of our ministry for many years. Often it's my joy to go to her home to visit with her and her husband. I consider Mrs. Mabel Chapman, now eighty-six years of age, one of the choice friends of my lifetime.

She indeed is a Christian who stands firmly against the fear Satan tries to bring into our lives.

THE FEAR OF FLYING

"I am scheduled to fly to visit my relatives in the East very soon. Frankly, I am not at all excited about it, because I have a dreadful fear of the prospect of flying in an airplane. This air flight seems frightening. I know, Brother Gossett, that you do a good deal of flying and traveling, and I'd like to have some words of encouragement from you to overcome this spirit of fear."

I am glad you wrote me at this time, because I know that I can help you to believe God's Word to possess safety in travel.

Many years ago, this truth of God became very precious to me, *"Safety is of the LORD"* (Proverbs 21:31).

When you really believe this Bible promise that safety is of the Lord, You will have no spirit of fear; you will possess confidence. Again the Bible says in Psalm 33:17, *"A horse is a vain thing for safety."* it can be paraphrased in this day that a car is a vain thing for safety, or that a jet plane is a vain thing for safety. Even your home is a vain thing for safety. Your safety is not in the locks on the door, or in the seat belts in the car or plane, but *your safety is truly in the Lord.* The Lord wants us to exercise wisdom and take proper precautionary measures to protect ourselves. But real safety is in Him.

Begin to confess that the Lord is your Protector against being in a plane accident. Confess that the eyes of the Lord are upon you wherever you go. Confess that you need have no fear because God will take care of you. Confess that God is protecting you, whether you are at home, or on an airplane. Here's a wonderful Scripture whereby God assures us of safety, both day and night. Proverbs 3:23: *"Then shalt thou walk in thy way safely, and thy foot shall not stumble. When thou liest down, thou shalt not be afraid: yea, thou shalt lie down, and thy sleep shall be sweet. Be not afraid of sudden fear…. The LORD shall be thy confidence, and shall keep thy foot from being taken."* You can put your name in each verse here in Proverbs 3 and confess it is yours, that you shall be kept safely, that your foot shall not be taken and you can praise the Lord.

Proverbs 1:33: *"Who so hearkeneth unto me shall dwell safely, an shall be quiet from the fear of evil."* Here God promises you that as you hearken unto Him, You will dwell safely.

Of course, the safety that is ours is in the name of the Lord. Remember Proverbs 18:10: *"The name of the LORD is a strong tower: the righteous runneth into it, and is safe."* Our safety is in the precious, wonderful name of our Lord Jesus Christ. Have great confidence in His name!

THE FEAR OF NATURE

The elements of nature can at times be frightening to people and cause not only undesirable results but also the continual harassment of fear. Mr. Arthur Thomas of Eckville, Alberta, wrote me about overcoming this particular type of fear.

"I have a testimony of Overcoming fear I've never shared before that interest you because it shows how standing on

God's Word can be so effective. We've had abnormal number of wasps in this area in the summer months for the past several years. Until 3 years ago, a wasp sting never gave me much concern other than the initial burning sensation, which soon passed away. However, during mid-summer 3 years ago, I received a sting and several minutes later the surrounding scenery became wavy and everything seemed to look yellow. Added to this was extreme difficulty in breathing, along with a horrible taste in, my mouth.

"I ended up collapsing on the ground for about 5 minutes. Eventually, I gained strength and got to my home. There, I was overtaken with extreme chills so that I had to take a hot bath. Within an hour things were back to normal.

"The same thing happened the following summer and then again last summer. By this time, I had developed a real fear of wasps and was living in dread daily of being stung again. Several friends had suggested having 'shots' as an antidote or else carrying pills to take if and when I was stung again.

"Somehow, I didn't feel this was the answer, and as a result, the Lord showed me these Scriptures:

> *He shall deliver thee in six troubles: yea, in seven there shall no evil touch thee. In famine he shall redeem thee from death: and in war from the power of the sword. Thou shalt be hid from the scourge of the tongue: neither shalt thou be afraid of destruction when it cometh. At destruction and famine thou shalt laugh: neither shalt thou be afraid of the beasts of the earth. For thou shalt be in league with the stones of the field and the beasts of the field shall be at peace with thee.*
>
> (Job 5:19-23)

"Another passage that really ministered to my heart was Psalm 8:4-9: '*What is man, that thou art mindful of him? And the Son of man, that thou visitest him? For thou hast made him a little lower than the angels, and hast crowned him with glory and honour. Thou madest him to have dominion over the works of thy hands; thou hast put all things under his feet: all sheep and oxen, yea, and the beast of the field; the fowl of the air, and the fish of the sea, and whatsoever passeth through the paths of the seas. Oh LORD, our LORD, how excellent is thy name in all the earth!*'"

Mr. Thomas continued, "Quite often knowing Scripture and putting it into practice are two different things. Being hearers of the Word is one thing, but also we are commanded to be doers.

"The Lord kept impressing me to claim these promises quoted above, and I did so. Yet, I could feel my flesh crawl and I would cringe when any of these little creatures came close. I was still fearful.

"This went on for several days, and then one day I 'accidentally' bumped a wasp nest with my head. Wasps don't appreciate this type of familiarity and immediately they were all around and bouncing off my bare head and face. I know the Lord arranged this for it forced me to face my fears with His courage. I immediately claimed my authority over the wasps in the name of Jesus. I never received a sting, praise God.

"My fear left. I still believed, however, that the only good wasp was a dead wasp, and I would go running for a pray can if one appeared. However, the Lord spoke to me to leave them alone as they were now leaving me alone. These events clearly revealed to me that faith is built by the Word of God, and when we act upon it, then fear has to go."

Reading Mr. Thomas's beautiful testimony reminded me of another brother in the Lord who had a similar experience with stinging bees. One day while mowing his lawn with a power mower, he struck a bee's nest. Immediately, the bees made formation to attack him. He simply spoke out, "Bees, I apologize for striking your nest. Please forgive me. But now, bees, I command you in the name of Jesus Christ to go away and leave me alone."

Indeed, the bees obeyed and my Christian brother received no stings from the formation of bees.

As I write these lines, I have been saved 36 years. In those times, I have had the immeasurable joy of claiming God's promises for protection. I want to share those promises with you.

1. Genesis 28:15: *"Behold, I am with thee, and will keep thee in all places whither thou, goest."*

2. Psalm 4:8: *"I will both lay me down in peace and sleep; for thou, LORD, only makest me dwell in safety."*

3. Proverbs 1:33: *"But whoso hearkeneth unto me shall dwell safely, and shall be quiet from fear of evil."*

4. Psalm 27:1: *"The LORD is my light and my salvation; whom shall I fear? The LORD is the strength of my life; of whom shall I be afraid?"*

5. Deuteronomy 33:12: *"The beloved of the LORD shall dwell in safety by him; and the LORD shall cover him all the day long."*

6. Psalm 9 1:11: *"He shall give his angels charge over thee, to keep thee in all thy ways."*

7. Proverbs 18:10: *"The name of the LORD is a strong tower: the righteous runneth into it, and is safe."*

8. Psalm 91:2: *"I will say of the* LORD, *He is my refuge and my fortress: my God, in him will I trust."*

9. 2 Timothy 1:12: *"I know whom I have believed, and am persuaded that he is able to keep that which I have committed unto him against that day."*

10. Psalm 138:7: *"Though I walk in the midst of trouble, thou wilt revive me: thou shalt stretch forth thine hand against the wrath of mine enemies, and thy right hand shall save me."*

11. Exodus 33:22: *"I will put thee in a cleft of the rock, and will cover thee with my hand."*

12. Psalm 91:1: *"He that dwelleth in the secret place of the Most High shall abide under the shadow of the Almighty."*

13. 1 Peter 3:13: *"And who is he that will harm you, if ye be followers of that which is good?"*

14. Psalm 125:2: *"As the mountains are round about Jerusalem, so the* LORD *is round about his people from henceforth even forever."*

15. Psalm 34:7: *"The angel of the* LORD *encampeth round about them that fear him, and delivereth them."*

16. Psalm 34:19: *"Many are the afflictions of the righteous: but the* LORD *delivereth him out of them all."*

SUMMARY: You can rejoice that *"the* LORD *fills you with strength and protects you wherever you go"* (Psalm 18:32).

15

STANDING AGAINST FEAR

Are *you* really serious about a life of blessing? A life free from fear? Then I want to share with you a way of achieving abundant life that has meant a great deal to me throughout my years as a Christian.

When I was a young man of 18, I was totally occupied with the pursuit to know Jesus and make Him known to others. How could I get to know the Lord better? How could my life really count for Him?

God answered the quest of my spirit by introducing me to a method of Bible study that was to enrich my life and make my ministry very effective for all the years ahead. One of the courses I was taking at Glad Tidings Bible Institute at the time was on Personal Evangelism. A requirement of this course was to memorize five new Bible verses each week.

I discovered that I loved this way of learning God's Word. God used this method of study of the Holy Scriptures to answer my heart's desire to know Him better. I *learned to know Him through His Word.*

Memorizing hundreds of Bible verses proved to be an invaluable experience. The Word ministered deeply in my life, and I was able to share that same inspiration with others. As I began to share these newly memorized Scriptures, I soon became an effective soul winner by God's grace. It is sharing the Word of God in witnessing and preaching that really bears fruit.

In the same manner, an excellent way to use the Word of God as your main "weapon against fear" is by memorizing that Word and implanting it deeply within your heart. You can fortify yourself against discouragement, depression and fear by memorizing outstanding Bible passages on related subjects. It will not only bring you comfort and strength, but you will also be able to minister to others who are bound up in fear.

I want to share with you fifty Scriptures against fear that I have personally selected for your inspiration.

HOW TO MEMORIZE THESE VERSES ON FEAR

Fifty verses might seem like a great many to commit to memory, but if you'll follow this simple plan, you can do it. First, you will need fifty 3 x 5 file cards. On each card you will write the selection to be memorized, and on the reverse side you'll write the reference. After you have completed this task, you will then be ready to start your memorization program.

Memorize one verse each day, with its reference. Keep repeating the verse until you can say it without looking at the card. Learn to give the reference without turning the card over. After you have done this, then turn the card over and learn to give the verse by looking only at the reference. Each day that you add a new verse, review the previous ones.

After you've memorized four or five verses, you'll proceed each day by turning all cards with the reference side up. You should be able to recite the verses from memory the moment you see the reference. Then turn all the cards over, with the verse side up. You should be able to give the reference the moment you see the verse.

The key to this memorization program is *review*. As you accumulate more cards and review them each day, your store of memorized verses will grow and grow.

BENEFITS OF MEMORIZING THESE VERSES

First, *you'll receive greater answers to prayer.* Jesus said very plainly that you can only receive answers to prayer as His Word abides in you. *"If ye answer abide in me, and my words abide in you, ye shall ask what ye will, and it shall be done unto you"* (John 15:7).

Second, *you'll have greater blessings of physical health.* "My son, attend to my words, incline thine ear unto my sayings. Let them not depart from thine eyes keep them in the midst of thine heart. For they are life unto those that find them, and health to all their flesh" (Proverbs 4:20-22).

Third, *you'll be able to wield the Sword of the Spirit with greater authority.* The reason Satan seeks to "brainwash" you into believing that you can't memorize these verses is because he knows that once you are equipped with the Sword of the Spirit, you'll be a powerful foe. When you have the Word of God in your mind and heart, the Holy Spirit can draw upon this bank of knowledge to rout Satan at every turn; *"...take... the sword of the Spirit, which is the word of God"* (Ephesians 6:17).

Fourth, *you'll be able to overcome fear and depression.* I ask all the people who serve with me in our ministry to memorize Scripture. Then I'm assured that there won't be any negative, fearful, gloomy spirits to contend with, no scared saints dragging their feet and hindering the work of God.

🗝 THE CONFESSION OF A VICTOR ✍

If you memorize one of these selections I daily, it will take you not quite two months. Because of the very human tendency to start well and finish poorly, I would suggest that you make the following affirmation often during your memorization program:

I can memorize God's wonderful Word!

God says I can—so I can!

No matter what I think of myself, I can do it!

Regardless of my age, I can memorize God's Word!

In spite of past failures, I can *now* memorize God's Word!

When it seems hard, I refuse to give up!

When it appears I am slipping, I know God is helping me!

"I will not forget thy word" (Psalm 119:16).

"I can do all things through Christ which strengtheneth me" (Philippians 4:13).

Why am I so sure? God makes me sure, that's why!

50 SCRIPTURES TO STAND AGAINST FEAR ✍

1. 2 Timothy 1:7: *"God hath not given us the spirit of fear; but of power, and of love, and of a sound mind."*

2. Hebrews 13:6: *"So that we may boldly say, The Lord is my helper, and I will not fear what man shall do unto me."*

3. Isaiah 41:10: *"Fear thou not; for I am with thee: be not dismayed; for I am thy God: I will strengthen thee; yea, I will uphold thee with the right hand of my righteousness."*

4. Isaiah 43:1: "*Fear not: for I have redeemed thee, I have called thee by name; thou art mine.*"

5. 1 John 4:18: "*There is no fear in love; but perfect love casteth out fear: because fear hath torment. He that feareth is not made perfect in love.*"

6. Proverbs 29:25: "*The fear of man bringeth a snare: but whoso putteth his trust in the LORD shall be safe.*"

7. Deuteronomy 31:6: "*Be strong and of a good courage, fear not, nor be afraid of them: for the LORD thy God, he it is that doth go with thee; he will not fail thee, nor forsake thee.*"

8. Psalm 27:3: "*Though a host should encamp against me, my heart shall not fear: though war rise against me, in this I will be confident.*"

9. Romans 8:15: "*For ye have not received the spirit of bondage again to fear; but ye have received the Spirit of adoption, whereby we cry, Abba, Father.*"

10. 2 Chronicles 20:15: "*Thus saith the LORD unto you, Be not afraid nor dismayed by reason of this great multitude, for the battle is not yours, but God's.*"

11. Proverbs 1:33: "*But whoso hearkeneth unto me shall dwell safely, and shall be quiet from fear of evil.*"

12. Proverbs 3:23-24: "*Then shalt thou walk in the way, safely, and thy foot shall not stumble. When thou liest down, thou shalt not be afraid: yea, thou shalt lie down, and they sleep shall be sweet.*"

13. Psalm 34:4: "*I sought the LORD, and he heard me, and delivered me from all my fears.*"

14. Psalm 23:4: *"Yea, though I walk through the valley of the shadow of death, I will fear no evil: for thou art with me; thy rod and thy staff they comfort me."*

15. Proverbs 3:25: *"Be not afraid of sudden fear, neither of the desolation of the wicked, when it cometh."*

16. Proverbs 10:24: *"The fear of the wicked, it shall come upon him: but the desire of the righteous shall be granted."*

17. Genesis 15:1: *"After these things the word of the LORD came unto Abram in a vision, saying, Fear not, Abram: I am thy shield, and thy exceeding great reward."*

18. Exodus 14:13: *"And Moses said unto the people, Fear ye not, stand still, and see the salvation of the LORD, which he will show to you today."*

19. Deuteronomy 1:21: *"Behold, the LORD thy God hath set the land before thee: Go up and possess it, as the LORD God of thy fathers hath said unto thee; fear not, neither be discouraged."*

20. Deuteronomy 3:22: *"Ye shall not fear them: for the LORD your God he shall fight for you."*

21. Deuteronomy 31:8: *"And the LORD, he it is that doth go before thee; he will be with thee: he will not fail thee, neither forsake thee: fear not, neither be dismayed."*

22. Joshua 8:1: *"And the LORD said unto Joshua, Fear not, neither be thou dismayed; take all the people of war with thee, and arise."*

23. Joshua 10:25: *"And Joshua said unto them, Fear not, nor be dismayed, be strong and of good courage: for thus shall the LORD do to all your enemies against whom you fight."*

24. 2 Kings 6:16: *"And he answered, Fear not; for they that be with us are more than they that be with them."*

25. 2 Chronicles 20-17: *"Ye shall not need to fight in this battle: set yourselves, stand ye still, and see the salvation of the LORD with you, O Judah and Jerusalem: fear not, nor be dismayed; tomorrow go out against them: for the LORD will be with you."*

26. Psalm 56:3: *"What time I am afraid, I will trust in thee."*

27. Psalm 56:4: *"In God I will praise his word, in God I have put my trust; I will not fear what flesh can do unto me."*

28. Isaiah 35:4: *"Say to them that are of a fearful heart, be strong, fear not: behold, your God will come with vengeance, even God with a recompense; he will come and save you."*

29. Isaiah 41:13: *"For I the LORD thy God will hold thy right hand, saying unto thee, Fear not; I will help thee."*

30. Jeremiah 46:27: *"But fear thou not, O my servant Jacob, and be not dismayed, O Israel for, behold, I will save thee from afar off, and they seed from-the land of their captivity; and Jacob shall return, and be in rest and at ease, and none shall make him afraid."*

31. Daniel 10:19: *"O man greatly beloved, fear not: peace be unto thee, be strong, yea, be strong. And when he had spoken unto me, I was strengthened, and said, let my lord speak; for thou has strengthened me."*

32. Joel 2:21: *"Fear not, O land; be glad and rejoice: for the LORD will do great things."*

33. Isaiah 44:8: *"Fear ye not, neither be afraid: have not I told thee from that time, and have declared it? Ye are even my*

witnesses. Is there a God beside me? Yea, there is no God; I know not any."

34. Matthew 10:31: "Fear ye not therefore, ye are of more value than many sparrows."

35. Luke 12:32: "Fear not, little flock; for it is your Father's good pleasure to give you the kingdom."

36. Revelation 1:10: "Fear none of those things which thou shalt suffer behold, the devil shall cast some of you into prison, that ye may be tried; and ye shall have tribulation ten days: be thou faithful unto death, and I will give thee a crown of life."

37. Philippians 1:14: "And, many of the brethren m the Lord, waxing confident by my bonds, are much more bold to speak the word without fear."

38. Matthew 8:26: "And he saith unto them, Why are ye fearful, O ye of little faith? Then he arose, and rebuked the winds and the sea; and there was a great calm."

39. Revelation 21:8: "But the fearful, and unbelieving, and the abominable, and murderers, and whoremonger, and sorcerers, and idolaters, and all liars, shall have their part in the lake, which burneth with, fire and brimstone: which is the second death."

40. Jeremiah 42:11: "Be not afraid of the king of Babylon, of whom ye are afraid; be not afraid of him, saith the LORD: for I am with you to save you, and to deliver you from his hand."

41. Psalm 91:5: "Thou shalt not be afraid for the terror by night; nor for the arrow that flieth by day."

42. Psalm 112:7: *"He shall not be afraid of evil tidings: his heart is fixed, trusting in the LORD."*

43. Leviticus 26:6: *"And I will give peace in the land, and ye shall lie down, and none shall make you afraid: and I will rid evil beasts out of the land, neither shall the sword go through your land."*

44. Luke 12:4: *"And I say unto you my friends, be not afraid of them that kill the body, and after that have no more than they can do."*

45. Job 5:21: *"Thou shalt be hid from the scourge of the tongue: neither shalt thou be afraid of destruction when it cometh."*

46. Matthew 14:27: *"But straightway Jesus spake unto them, saying, be of good cheer; it is I; be not afraid."*

47. Mark 5:36: *"As soon as Jesus heard the word that was spoken, he saith unto the ruler of the synagogue, be not afraid, only believe."*

48. Joshua 1:9: *"Have I not commanded thee? Be strong and of a good courage; be not afraid, neither be thou dismayed: for the LORD thy God is with thee whithersoever thou goest."*

49. Isaiah 12:2: *"Behold, God is my salvation; I will trust, and not be afraid: for the LORD JEHOVAH is my strength and my song; he also is become my salvation."*

50. John 14:27: *"Peace I leave with you, my peace I give unto you: not as the world giveth, give I unto you. Let not your heart be troubled, neither let it be afraid."*

Amen.

16

THE CONQUEST OF FEAR AND WORRY

I would like to conclude our study on the subject of fear with a challenge from Forrest E. Smith, a pastor from Arkansas "We are living in the closing days of time. Even if we ministers never mentioned it, doubtless many would realize it because of the terrible oppression of observation of the enemy, and through appalling acts of sin openly flaunted before our conscience-seared nation.

"The battle between spirit and flesh has reached such a screaming pitch that even once stable Christians are floundering, being deceived or overpowered by the world. As nations pitted against each other work secretly to develop new weapons of horror, each struggling to produce the most devastating bomb or chemical, so the legions of darkness feverishly work against time bringing spiritual weapons to bear against the children of God. Into this bitter death struggle the devil has injected his most demoralizing weapon of the ages: FEAR!

"Several years ago I heard a friend say, 'I don't know what is wrong with me, but I have a feeling of dread in my soul. There is fear in my heart!' At that time, I thought that the Holy Spirit was sending conviction into his heart and that he needed to repent. I know now that my judgment was critical and unjust. My friend was being oppressed by a spirit of fear.

"Many people are being confused in these hours. We need to realize that there is a great deal of difference between Holy Spirit conviction and evil spirit oppression. If the Holy Spirit convicts us, the heaviness of heart will depart when we have repented of the hasty word or thoughtless action that brought the conviction. God's Word plainly says, '*If we confess our sins, he is faithful and just to forgive us our sins, and to cleanse us from all unrighteousness*' (1 John 1:9).

"However, after we are cleansed, the enemy may come along to dig up the matter again and oppress us, with a spirit of fear for our very salvation; he may cause us to doubt our baptism in the Holy Spirit, or our healing. We may find ourselves pleading for forgiveness that was granted long ago. This is a spirit of fear and should be recognized and combated as such. It is the oppression of the devil.

"Such oppression drives men and women to destroy themselves in despair. It causes them to mistrust each other, to doubt God and His Word, to question the reality of salvation and spiritual things. This oppression is a sharp, terrifying, accusing voice that threatens to smother prayer under a blanket of unbelief. And it is not from God!

"For '*God hath not given us the spirit of fear; but of power, and of love, and of a sound mind*' (2 Timothy 1:7). *God has given us the spirit of power!*

"Power over what? '*Behold*,' Jesus said to the disciples, '*I give you power...over all the power of the enemy*' (Luke 10:19).

"In Acts 1:18, we learn that we shall receive power to witness. In 1 John 4:4, we learn that we are of God and have already overcome the devil, for greater is he that is in us than he that is in the world. A person who is saved has already overcome the devil to the extent of being saved. If we can overcome the devil on one front, we can overcome him on all fronts.

"God told Joshua, 'No man shall be able to stand before you all the days of your life!' And we have that same God within our hearts! Only now we have better promises and a more sure word of testimony than had Joshua! If Joshua under the law could be strong and of good courage, how much more shall we who are under grace? For God has not given us the spirit of fear, but of power! Power to work, power to witness and power to overcome the devil on every hand!

"And God has given us the spirit of love!

"Love is not one of our natural attributes. It is an attribute of God—'God is love.' Galatians 5:22 tells us that love is a fruit of the indwelling Spirit of Christ. Love is a powerful force, greater then anything the devil has concocted. Love is the way to conquer fear, for 'perfect love casteth out all fear.' Not that we cease to reverence God, but that we cease to fear judgment on sins that have already been judged!

"Love covers a multitude of sins. It covered our sins with Jesus's blood and washed them away completely, so that there is no longer any record of them in heaven. And that same love will help us to be patient with a lot of things our loved ones and fellow Christians do! We won't mind the off key singing by some anointed but untalented saint! We won't seek promotion for 'love vaunteth not itself.' We won't be proud of our small accomplishments, for *'love is not puffed up.'* God has not given us the spirit of fear, but of love!

"*And God has given us the spirit of a sound mind!*

"With the spirit of a sound mind we will recognize the tactics of the devil and will measure every vision and revelation by the Word of God. A sound mind will realize that the 'extra touch' required in the pulpit is simply more of God's Spirit and not some spectacular program hatched up to exalt man and draw greater crowds. Paul said in 2 Corinthians 2:11, *'We are not ignorant of [Satan's] devices.'* We are aware that we fight against principalities and powers with which God alone can cope. Let us then stay clear of unscriptural and unsound practices, and let us live by the revealed truth of God. Therefore, when the enemy comes in like a flood, let God lift up a standard against him! When he seeks to oppress with the spirit of fear, don't remain passive rebuke him! Don't spend a lot of time arguing with him, for God has given us authority over the situation. God has given us the perfect antidote for fear. *It is the spirit of power, and of love, and of a sound mind!*"

As a summary, just remember the following and move on to rise above fear and live in total victory!

Just remember:

1. Fear has one source, the devil: *"For God hath not given us the spirit of fear; but of power, and of love, and of a sound mind"* (2 Timothy 1:7).

2. Notice that fear is not a 'mental quirk, but an actual spirit that emanates, not from God, but from the adversary: *"For ye have not received the spirit of bondage again to fear"* (Romans 8:15).

3. The results of fear are not pleasant. In fact, fear produces deep discomfort: *"Fear hath torment"* (1 John 4:18). Victims of satanic fear actually suffer physical agony, mental anguish, and spiritual torment.

4. Further, fear is deceptive; it leads people into snares of the enemy: *"The fear of man bringeth a snare"* (Proverbs 29:25). Fear leads astray, beguiles, deludes, and leads people into a make-believe world of deception.

5. Fear produces in kind. You fear cancer, and that spirit of fear can actually produce cancer. Fear calamity, and you can be writing your own ticker for calamity. Fear failure, and you are opening the door for failure to envelope your life. Dare to rebuke fear in the name of Jesus. Call the spirit of fear by its right names: a deceiver, a liar, a faker, and a fraud. *"Resist the devil, and he will flee from you"* (James 4:7).

6. Fear causes you to expect the bad. It can lead to an urge to commit suicide. Fear is manifested in stinginess towards God in your giving. Fear creates nervous breakdowns, sleeplessness, and oppression in your prayer life and bondage in witnessing.

7. No more convincing testimony is on record than that of Job, how "the thing which he feared came upon him, and that which he was afraid of came unto him." Defeat, depression, destruction and even death were the results of his fears! Give no place to fear. Resist it in Jesus's name. Plead the blood. Quote the Word. Praise the Lord!

ABOUT THE AUTHOR

Don Gossett (1929–2014) served the Lord through full-time ministry for more than fifty years. Born again at the age of twelve, Don answered his call to the ministry just five years later and began by reaching out to his unsaved family members. Don apprenticed with many well-known evangelists, including William Freeman, Raymond T. Richey, Jack Coe, and T. L. Osborn. Don's writings have been translated into eighteen languages, with more than 25 million copies in print. His acclaimed daily radio broadcast, *Bold Bible Living*, began in 1961 and was heard in eighty-nine nations over the years. As a missionary evangelist, Don personally ministered in sixty-five nations with signs and wonders following the Word of God. Don raised five children with his first wife, Joyce, who went to be with the Lord in 1991. In 1995, Don wed his second wife, Debra. She was also called to the Lord's service and continues Don's work with the Don Gossett Ministries.